First World War
and Army of Occupation
War Diary
France, Belgium and Germany

3 CAVALRY DIVISION
Divisional Troops
Royal Army Veterinary Corps
20 Mobile Veterinary Section
1 March 1915 - 26 February 1918

WO95/1149/4

The Naval & Military Press Ltd
www.nmarchive.com
Published in association with The National Archives

Published by

The Naval & Military Press Ltd

Unit 10 Ridgewood Industrial Park,

Uckfield, East Sussex,

TN22 5QE England

Tel: +44 (0) 1825 749494

www.naval-military-press.com

www.nmarchive.com

This diary has been reprinted in facsimile from the original. Any imperfections are inevitably reproduced and the quality may fall short of modern type and cartographic standards.

© Crown Copyright
Images reproduced by permission of The National Archives, London, England, 2015.

Contents

Document type	Place/Title	Date From	Date To
Heading	WO95/1149/4		
Heading	1915-1918 3rd Cavalry Division 20th Mobile Vety Section Mar 1915-Feb 1918		
Heading	War Diary of 20th Mobile Vet. Section 3rd Cavalry Division March-December-1915 to Feb 1918		
Heading	3rd Cavalry Division 20th Mobile Vety. Section Vol I 1-31.3.15		
War Diary	Woolwich	01/03/1915	01/03/1915
War Diary	Southampton	01/03/1915	03/03/1915
War Diary	S S Maidan	04/03/1915	04/03/1915
War Diary	Havre	05/03/1915	08/03/1915
War Diary	In Train Steenebecque	09/03/1915	09/03/1915
War Diary	Ebblinghem	09/03/1915	11/03/1915
War Diary	Surcus	12/03/1915	12/03/1915
War Diary	Sec Bois	12/03/1915	13/03/1915
War Diary	Ebblinghem	14/03/1915	14/03/1915
War Diary	Renescure	15/03/1915	31/03/1915
Miscellaneous	Nominal Roll-No. 20 Mobile Vety Sec		
Miscellaneous	No 20 Mobile Veterinary Section		
Heading	3rd Cavalry Division 20th Mobile Vety. Section Vol II 1-30.4.15		
War Diary	Renescure	01/04/1915	05/04/1915
War Diary	Wallon Cappel	06/04/1915	06/04/1915
War Diary	Ebblinghem	06/04/1915	07/04/1915
War Diary	Renescure	07/04/1915	11/04/1915
War Diary	La Carnois	12/04/1915	25/04/1915
War Diary	Surcus	23/04/1915	23/04/1915
War Diary	La Carnois	24/04/1915	24/04/1915
War Diary	Surcus	25/04/1915	30/04/1915
Heading	3rd Cavalry Division 20th Mobile Vety. Section Vol III May 15		
War Diary	Abeele	01/05/1915	01/05/1915
War Diary	Blaringhem	02/05/1915	03/05/1915
War Diary	Abeele	04/05/1915	04/05/1915
War Diary	Houtkerque	04/05/1915	04/05/1915
War Diary	Blaringhem	04/05/1915	07/05/1915
War Diary	La Carnois	08/05/1915	22/05/1915
War Diary	Vlamertinghe	22/05/1915	22/05/1915
War Diary	Reninghelst	22/05/1915	23/05/1915
War Diary	Pradelles	23/05/1915	23/05/1915
War Diary	La Carnois	23/05/1915	31/05/1915
Heading	3rd Cavalry Division 20th Mobile Vety. Section Vol IV June 1915		
War Diary	La Carnois	01/06/1915	30/06/1915
Heading	3rd Cavalry Division 20th Mobile Vety Section Vol V July 15		
War Diary	La Carnois	01/07/1915	30/07/1915
Heading	3rd Cavalry Division 20th Mobile Vety. Section Vol VI August 15		
War Diary	La Carnois	01/08/1915	06/08/1915

War Diary	Petigny	07/08/1915	31/08/1915
Heading	3rd Cavalry Division 20th Mobile Vety. Section Vol VII Sept. 15		
War Diary	Petigny	01/09/1915	21/09/1915
War Diary	Westrehem	22/09/1915	27/09/1915
War Diary	Noeux Les Mines	28/09/1915	29/09/1915
War Diary	Gosnay	30/09/1915	30/09/1915
Heading	3rd Cavalry Division 20th Mobile Vety. Section Vol VIII Oct 15		
War Diary	Gosnay	01/10/1915	01/10/1915
War Diary	Ladeuvriere	02/10/1915	03/10/1915
War Diary	Burbure	04/10/1915	19/10/1915
War Diary	Reclinghem	20/10/1915	31/10/1915
Heading	3rd Cavalry Division 20 Mob. Vet. Sec. Nov. 1915 Vol IX		
War Diary	Beaumetz Les Aire	01/11/1915	17/11/1915
War Diary	Rimboval	17/11/1915	30/11/1915
Heading	Dec-1915 20th Mobile Vet Section		
War Diary	Rimboval	01/12/1915	31/05/1916
War Diary	Loison	31/05/1916	31/05/1916
War Diary	Brimeux	31/05/1916	31/05/1916
War Diary	Merlimont	31/05/1916	31/05/1916
Miscellaneous	Appendix 8th Cavalry Brigade	11/05/1916	11/05/1916
War Diary	Merlimont	01/06/1916	10/06/1916
War Diary	Rimboval	11/06/1916	24/06/1916
War Diary	Regniere Ecluse	25/06/1916	25/06/1916
War Diary	St Ouen	26/06/1916	26/06/1916
War Diary	Bonnay	27/06/1916	30/06/1916
Miscellaneous	Supply and Requisitioning Officer, 8th Cav. Bde. 2/Lt. Hann Royal Horse Guards.	23/06/1916	23/06/1916
Miscellaneous	Distribution As B.M. 714/3 App B	25/06/1916	25/06/1916
Miscellaneous	Bm 714/6		
Miscellaneous	Bm 714/5 App C	26/06/1916	26/06/1916
War Diary	Bonnay	01/07/1916	04/07/1916
War Diary	Bailleul	05/07/1916	08/07/1916
War Diary	Corbie	09/07/1916	09/07/1916
War Diary	Bonnay	10/07/1916	01/08/1916
War Diary	Pipierrea Gouy	02/08/1916	02/08/1916
War Diary	Nevilly L'Hopital	03/08/1916	04/08/1916
War Diary	Douriez	05/08/1916	05/08/1916
War Diary	Blingel	06/08/1916	10/09/1916
War Diary	Douriez	10/09/1916	11/09/1916
War Diary	St. Riquier	12/09/1916	12/09/1916
War Diary	St. Sauveur	13/09/1916	14/09/1916
War Diary	Bussy Les Daours	14/09/1916	15/09/1916
War Diary	La Neuville	16/09/1916	17/09/1916
War Diary	Vecquemont	17/09/1916	22/09/1916
War Diary	L'Etoile	23/09/1916	23/09/1916
War Diary	Rougefay	23/09/1916	24/09/1916
War Diary	Bois Jean	25/09/1916	30/09/1916
Miscellaneous	Appendix A	09/09/1916	09/09/1916
Miscellaneous	App. B	10/09/1916	10/09/1916
Miscellaneous	App. C	11/09/1916	11/09/1916
Miscellaneous	App. D	13/09/1916	13/09/1916
Miscellaneous	App. "E"	14/09/1916	14/09/1916
Miscellaneous	App. F	17/09/1916	17/09/1916

Miscellaneous	App. "G"	21/09/1916	21/09/1916
Miscellaneous	App H	22/09/1916	22/09/1916
Miscellaneous	App. "J"		
War Diary	Beaurain	01/10/1916	01/10/1916
War Diary	Chateau	02/10/1916	02/10/1916
War Diary	Brimeux	03/10/1916	26/10/1916
War Diary	Hesmond	27/10/1916	22/12/1916
War Diary	Cucq	23/12/1916	31/12/1916
Miscellaneous	App. A	21/12/1916	21/12/1916
Miscellaneous	Unit in Order of March		
War Diary	Cucq	01/01/1917	01/02/1917
War Diary	Planques	01/02/1917	28/02/1917
Miscellaneous	App. A	28/01/1917	28/01/1917
Miscellaneous	March Table		
War Diary	Planques	01/03/1917	31/03/1917
Miscellaneous	App. A	19/03/1917	19/03/1917
War Diary	Planques	01/04/1917	05/04/1917
War Diary	Fressin	06/04/1917	07/04/1917
War Diary	Frevent	07/04/1917	08/04/1917
War Diary	Gouy en Artois	08/04/1917	18/04/1917
War Diary	Remaisnil	18/04/1917	19/04/1917
War Diary	Jumel	20/04/1917	30/04/1917
Miscellaneous	App. A	08/04/1917	08/04/1917
War Diary	Jumel	01/05/1917	13/05/1917
War Diary	Vaulx	14/05/1917	14/05/1917
War Diary	Frohen Le Grand	14/05/1917	15/05/1917
War Diary	Talmas	15/05/1917	16/05/1917
War Diary	Querrieu	16/05/1917	17/05/1917
War Diary	Hamel	17/05/1917	19/05/1917
War Diary	Herbecourt	19/05/1917	19/05/1917
War Diary	Courcelles	19/05/1917	31/05/1917
Miscellaneous	App. A	12/05/1917	12/05/1917
Miscellaneous	March Table		
Miscellaneous	App. B	13/05/1917	13/05/1917
Miscellaneous	Billets have been allotted for Billeting Area 14/5/17 as follow	15/05/1917	15/05/1917
Miscellaneous	App. C	16/05/1917	16/05/1917
Miscellaneous	Remarks		
Miscellaneous	App.D	15/05/1917	15/05/1917
Miscellaneous	March Table		
Miscellaneous	App. E	16/05/1917	16/05/1917
Miscellaneous	March Table		
Miscellaneous	App. F	18/05/1917	18/05/1917
Miscellaneous	March Table-19.5.17		
War Diary	Courcelles	01/06/1917	02/07/1917
War Diary	Suzanne	02/07/1917	03/07/1917
War Diary	Heilly	03/07/1917	04/07/1917
War Diary	Orville	04/07/1917	05/07/1917
War Diary	Etree Wamin	05/07/1917	06/07/1917
War Diary	Dieval	06/07/1917	17/07/1917
War Diary	Thiennes	17/07/1917	31/07/1917
Miscellaneous	App. A	30/06/1917	30/06/1917
Miscellaneous	App. B	02/07/1917	02/07/1917
Miscellaneous	Amplier 4 Etree Wamin		
Miscellaneous	App. C	03/07/1917	03/07/1917
Miscellaneous	3rd Cavalry Division (For information) App. D	04/07/1917	04/07/1917

Type	Description	Date From	Date To
Miscellaneous	March Table For July 5th, 1917		
Miscellaneous	App. E.	05/07/1917	05/07/1917
Miscellaneous	Movement Table For July 6th, 1917		
Miscellaneous	App. F. 3rd Cavalry Division (For information)	15/07/1917	15/07/1917
Miscellaneous	March Table For July 17th.		
War Diary	Thiennes	01/08/1917	10/08/1917
War Diary	Ham En Artois	11/08/1917	11/10/1917
War Diary	Rue De Guarbecque	12/10/1917	17/10/1917
War Diary	Pressy Les Pernes	18/10/1917	21/10/1917
War Diary	Rebreuve	21/10/1917	22/10/1917
War Diary	Vignacourt	23/10/1917	31/10/1917
Operation(al) Order(s)	8th Cavalry Brigade Order No.4 App. A	10/10/1917	10/10/1917
Miscellaneous	March Table For October 11th, 1917		
Operation(al) Order(s)	8th Cavalry Brigade Order No. 5. App B	16/10/1917	16/10/1917
Miscellaneous	March Table-October 17th, 1917		
Operation(al) Order(s)	8th Cavalry Brigade Order No.6 App. C.	20/10/1917	20/10/1917
Miscellaneous	March Table October 21st, 1917		
Operation(al) Order(s)	8th Cavalry Brigade Order No.7 App. D	20/10/1917	20/10/1917
Miscellaneous	March Table October 22nd, 1917		
War Diary	Vignacourt	05/11/1917	18/11/1917
War Diary	Bray	22/11/1917	23/11/1917
War Diary	Bertangles	26/11/1917	02/12/1917
War Diary	Belloy	18/12/1917	25/12/1917
War Diary	Belloy Sur Somme	01/01/1918	27/01/1918
War Diary	Marcelcave	28/01/1918	28/01/1918
War Diary	Meraucourt	10/02/1918	26/02/1918

WO 95/1149/4

1915-1918
3RD CAVALRY DIVISION

20TH MOBILE VETY SECTION
MAR 1915 - FEB 1918

WAR DIARY

OF

20TH MOBILE VET. SECTION.

3RD CAVALRY DIVISION

MARCH – DECEMBER – 1915.
to
Feb. 1916

3rd Cavalry Division

20th Mobile Vety: Section

Vol I. 1 — 31.3.15.

WAR DIARY or INTELLIGENCE SUMMARY

Army Form C. 2118.

No 20 Mobile Vety Section
8th Cav. Bde.

Place	Date	Hour	Summary of Events and Information	Remarks and references to Appendices
WOOLWICH	1.3.15	9.30.a.m	Left by train with Section * Rain No 10.	*Nominal roll written Appendix No 1
SOUTHAMPTON	1.3.15	1.45.p.m	Entrained & Limbers turned in on board S.S. MAIDAN	
		2 p.m	Left quay side for REST CAMPS remained there for the night – Horses picketed under trees. Men sleeping in the open. – O.C. billeted at CENTRAL HOTEL	
	2.3.15	6 a.m	Paraded all day marching orders to embark – orders given to sergeants in charge at 6 p.m. to be at quayside by 2.15. March 3. 1915.	
	3.3.15	6 a.m	Preparing to move to quay.	
		1 p.m	Loading up & left REST CAMP for quayside. Horses & limbers straight away.	
		2.15.p.m	All aboard fit & well. Big boat but ventilation very bad – No further incident.	
S.S. MAIDAN	4.3.15	6 a.m	Left by the quayside – Men allowed off the boat for exercise for two hours in the morning.	
		3 p.m	Brigade Major & M. Staff Officer came round for particulars of the unit & the General of the Brigade inspected the boat – fire alarm (practice)	
		2.30.p.m	Left quayside. Proceeded down estuary – Sun shining no incident on up the Spithead – Proceeded across channel as on a night march – Sea quite calm – Horses quite fit but short of air	
HAVRE	5.3.15	7 a.m	Arrived in mouth of river outside HAVRE	
		2 p.m	Arrived in dock. Proceeded to disembark	

WAR DIARY or INTELLIGENCE SUMMARY.

Army Form C. 2118.

No. 20 Mobile Vety Sec Army
6th Cav. Div.

Place	Date	Hour	Summary of Events and Information	Remarks and references to Appendices
HAVRE	5.3.15	4 p.m.	All safely disembarked — drew rifles & revolvers from Ordnance Store on Quay, & then marched with guide to No 1 REST CAMP	
"		6 a.m.	No 1 RESTCAMP — Bleak cold spot — Horses picketted in the open change after stuffy ship — night bitterly cold — the horses with temperatures — had tents for myself men	
"	6.3.15	6 a.m.	Standing to, awaiting orders to march up country — Horses behaved as a whole very fair — picked for train from Ordnance office (26).	
"	7.3.15	6 a.m.	Standing to awaiting orders — drew tents, haney traces from Ordnance — learned that we should probably move up country next day — Received horses over.	
"	8.3.15	12 noon	Received orders to be at Station GARE DE MARCHADAISE at 3.30 p.m.	
"		3.30 p.m.	Arrived at station drew rations for 3 days & entrained.	
"		7 p.m.	Left station & travelled all night.	
On Train		@ 3.15		
Steenbecque	"	2.30 p.m.	Arrived & detrained immediately — met by Sergeant of M.M.P. & one transport wagon sent by Brig. Ad. Q to conduct us to our billets — Very thoughtful.	
EBBLINGHEM	9.3.15	6 p.m.	Arrived at billets in a farm — Reported arrival to Bde. Maj. in person & writing & also in writing to A.D.V.S. 3rd Cav. Div. including nominal rolls in each case. Horses their pickets more in two ranks one unparked very little straw	

1577 Wt W:o7791/1773 500,000 1/15 D. D. & L. A.D.S.S./Forms/C. 2118.

WAR DIARY or INTELLIGENCE SUMMARY

Army Form C. 2118.

No 20 Mob. Vety Sec
(No. Sou Roll)

Place	Date	Hour	Summary of Events and Information	Remarks and references to Appendices
EBBLINGHEM	10.3.15	6 a.m.	Remained in billets nearly [?] an about retire – Exercised horses a little in vicinity – Reveille	
		8 a.m.	Interpreter Byur arrived + was away in evening taking a horse –	
			Raining [?] to be so [?] SURCUS in rear of Echelon B by 9 a.m. – Packed everything ready for early move.	
EBBLINGHEM	11.3.15	4 a.m.	Reveille	
		6 a.m.	Moved out of billets + arrived at SURCUS as ordered –	
		8 a.m.	Lieut A.D.V.S. + collected horses (14) off Echelon B + 12 horses left behind by the Royal Horse Guards at [?] –	
		11 a.m.	Proceeded with sick horses to STEENEBECQUE – Entrained horses + rank [?] when Echelon B had gone to – Supply Officer said that Echelon B still at [?] as mentioned time –	
SURCUS		11 a.m.	No returns arrived	
SORCUS	12.3.15	6 a.m.	Standing to – Called on 13 Mob Vety Sec. + learnt something of this returns that had to be furnished	
		1 p.m.	Made out returns in return – Knew nature for previous day.	
		1.30 p.m.	Received pahre horse in rear of Echelon B to SEC. BOIS.	
SEC. BOIS.	12.3.15	5 p.m.	Visited Base H.Q. [?] [?] to be issued for regiments to evacuate horses to our billets during the night – 13 horses arrived.	

WAR DIARY
or
INTELLIGENCE SUMMARY.
(Erase heading not required.)

Army Form C. 2118.

No 20 Mob. Vety. Sec
6th Cav. Bde

Instructions regarding War Diaries and Intelligence Summaries are contained in F. S. Regs., Part II. and the Staff Manual respectively. Title pages will be prepared in manuscript.

Place	Date	Hour	Summary of Events and Information	Remarks and references to Appendices
SEC BOIS	13.3.15	—	Standing to — Evacuated 13 horses from HAZEBROUCK —	
	"	12 noon	Officer return from HAZEBROUCK received note from V.O. Royal Horse Guards that he had ten horses for evacuation —	
	"	5 p.m	Went round to H.Q. of Royal Horse Guards to collect horses but found they had left with remounts from Billets	
	"	6.30 p.m	Section left for new billets at EBBLINGHEM	
EBBLINGHEM	14.3.15	—	Collected 5 horses from Roy. Horse Gds.	
	"	12 noon	Moved into billets at RENESCURE — Very good billets for horses & men.	
RENESCURE	15.3.15		Kept Standing to all day ready to move at short notice — Collected horses & dispatched 8 from EBBLINGHEM STATION — Had horses left by 3.30. A train — Much letter food dragging sick horses eight mile along the road to a railhead. —	*Appendix B No 2
RENESCURE	16.3.15	—	Routine work *	
"	17.3.15	—	Routine	
"	18.3.15	—	Routine	
"	19.3.15	—	Routine — Sent 8 sick horses to NEUFCHATEL from EBBLINGHEM STATION	
"	20.3.15	—	Routine	

WAR DIARY
or
INTELLIGENCE SUMMARY.

(Erase heading not required.)

Army Form C. 2118.

No 20 Mob. Vety Sec
& No Cav. Rec

Place	Date	Hour	Summary of Events and Information	Remarks and references to Appendices
RENESCURE	21.3.15	—	Routine work	
"	22.3.15	—	Routine work.	
"	23.3.15	—	Evacuated 7 horses EBBLINGHEM to NEUFCHATEL — Stock now in full size chg of R.C.I. Ruxman	JPB
"	24.3.15	—	X Royal Hussars evacuated to Remounts Depot, BOULOGNE. 6th Hrs evacuated to ESSEX YEOMANRY. Essex Yeomanry	JPB
"	25.3.15	—	Routine.	JPB
"	26.3.15	—	Routine — Myself & 14 men inoculated against enteric fever — I have evacuated to H.Q. 8th Bgde.	JPB
"	27.3.15	—	Men complain of being unwell as the results of inoculation — Seem to think that they are entitled to 48 hours exc'd duty — Eat & sleep well — Inspected horses of 7 Cav. Fd. Ambulance. & find them firm in condition. On return to billets find A.D.V.S. Cav. Corps & A.D.V.S. 3rd Cav. Div. taking an informal inspection. Unfortunate time for an inspection as men laying about complaining that they feel ill & little work done. A.D.V.S. thought that the men were only feigning illness — Very difficult to say.	JPB
"	28.3.15	—	Routine — 5 horses evacuated to NEUFCHATEL from EBBLINGHEM.	JPB
"	29.3.15	—	Routine — S.E. 3920 Pte. WOODS & S.E. 3864 Pte. NEWMAN J.H. start work in the forge.	JPB
"	30.3.15	—	Routine —	JPB

Army Form C. 2118.

WAR DIARY
or
INTELLIGENCE SUMMARY.
(Erase heading not required.)

No 20 Mob. Vety Sec.
& One Pill

Instructions regarding War Diaries and Intelligence Summaries are contained in F. S. Regs., Part II. and the Staff Manual respectively. Title pages will be prepared in manuscript.

[Stamp: NO. 20 MOBILE VETERINARY SECTION]

Place	Date	Hour	Summary of Events and Information	Remarks and references to Appendices
RENESCURE	21.3.18	—	Routine.	

1577 Wt.W10791/1773 500,000 1/15 D.D. & L. A.D.S.S./Forms/C. 2118.

Nominal Roll.   Appendix No I.
No 20 Mobile Vety Sec.

342	Sergt. Squires H	Lieut. S.J. Davis A.V.C.
269	Sergt. Mansfield W	
S.E. 4670	A/Cpl. Messer H	
" 4161	Pte Atkinson J	
" 4177	Pte Belcher J	
" 3865	Pte Belsham H	
" 3977	Pte Cunliffe A.C.	
" 3871	Pte Dean P.	
" 3661	Pte Griffiths J	
" 4162	Pte King A.H.	
" 4449	Pte Laidman S.	
" 2091	Pte McIntyre J.	
" 3864	Pte Newman J.H	
" 3606	Pte Phillips R.	
" 3496	Pte Scruby S.H.	
" 3866	Pte Selves A.W	
" 3869	Pte Smith F.C.	
" 3992	Pte Tamblin F.E.	
" 3211	Pte Welby W	
" 4133	Pte Williams W.R.	
" 3063	Pte Wilson R.J.	
" 3920	Pte Woods H.J.	
" 4093	Pte Woodward H.	
" 3666	Pte Broomfield P.	
35413	Dr Elliott H. }	No 2 Transport Company A.S.C.
35408	Dr Stonehouse G. }	Attached

J. Davis
Lieut., A.V.C.
O.C. No. 20 Mob. Sect. A.V.C.

NO. 20 MOBILE VETERINARY SECTION

Appendix No 2. Routine.   No 20 Mobile Vety Section.

- 6. a.m. Reveille
- 6.30. am Stables
- 7.15. a.m. Water & Feed.
- 7.30. a.m. Breakfast.
- 8.30 Exercise
- 10 a.m Return from exercise – Stables
- 12.30. p.m. Water & feed
- 12.45 p.m. Rifle inspection
- 1 p.m. Dinners
- 2.30 – 4.30 Fatigues, Lectures. Grazing. etc
- 4.30 p.m Stables.
- 5. p.m. Water & feed.
- 5.15 p.m. Teas
- 6 p.m. Night Guard posted
- 7.30 p.m. Hay up.
- 9.30 p.m Lights out.

J P Davy
Lieut A.V.C.
O.C. 20 Mob. Vety Sec.

187/5610

end

3rd Cavalry Division

20th Inf.Div. Sector

Vol III. 1 — 30.4.15.

WAR DIARY
or
INTELLIGENCE SUMMARY.

(Erase heading not required.)

Army Form C. 2118.

No. 20 Mob. Vety Sec
8th Cav. Bde

Instructions regarding War Diaries and Intelligence Summaries are contained in F. S. Regs., Part II. and the Staff Manual respectively. Title pages will be prepared in manuscript.

Place	Date	Hour	Summary of Events and Information	Remarks and references to Appendices
RENESCURE	1.4.15	—	Routine work.	
"	2.4.15	—	Routine work. Evacuated 7 sick horses to NEUFCHATEL for EBBLINGHEM.	
"	3.4.15	—	Routine	
"	4.4.15	—	Routine	
"	5.4.15	—	Routine — Received orders to move Section to the farm ½ mile N. of N. in WALLON CAPPEL (Ref Map Hazebrouck 5A) by 12 noon 6.4.15. to make room for French Troops.	Ref Map HAZEBROUCK 5A
WALLON CAPPEL	6.4.15 12 noon		Move completed but farm occupied by Life Guards — Received orders to take Section to farm on EBBLINGHEM – LYNDE road.	
EBBLINGHEM	6.4.15 6 p.m.		Move completed — Very dirty billet + little accommodation.	
EBBLINGHEM	7.4.15		Made efforts to make this billet more respectable, weather difficult — Received staff offr. 5th Cav. Bde to allow me to move Section back to RENESCURE.	
RENESCURE	7.4.15 4 p.m.		Move completed.	
"	8.4.15	—	Routine work	
"	9.4.15	—	Routine. 8 horses sent from EBBLINGHEM to NEUFCHATEL	No 3666. BROOMFIELD Pte Broomfield reported sick. Sent to 8th Cav. Fd Ambulance at Boulevard
"	10.4.15	—	Routine work	
"	11.4.15	—	Routine — Received orders to move Section to farm 1 kilometre NNW of L.A. CARNOIS. by 12 noon. 12.4.15. 8 horses evacuated EBBLINGHEM to NEUFCHATEL.	

WAR DIARY
or
INTELLIGENCE SUMMARY.

Army Form C. 2118.

No 20 Mob Vety Sec
8th Cav. Bde.

Place	Date	Hour	Summary of Events and Information	Remarks and references to Appendices
LA CARNOIS.	12.4.15	12 noon	Move complete — Inspected by A.D.V.S. 3rd Cav. Div.	
"	"	2 p.m.	Proceeded to RENESCURE & placed two teams out of bounds on account of sick horses.	
"	"		Having been billeted there with a regt.	
"	"	6 p.m.	Sub referred to A.D.V.S. — Received orders to move farther down the road in direction of LA CARNOIS.	
"	13.4.15		Preparing for inspection by A.D.V.S. Cav. Corps. at 11 a.m. Very little information necessary.	
"	"	11.6. a.m.	Paraded on road outside billet — Raining hard.	
"	"	2 p.m.	No sign of A.D.V.S. so ordered section into the new billets just west of the L. in LA CARNOIS. — Expected to hear reason of absence of A.D.V.S.	
LA CARNOIS	14.4.15		Routine. New billets quite good.	
"	15.4.15		Routine.	
"	16.4.15		Routine. — Received orders not to evacuate horses except from stations where RTOs are on duty.	
"	17.4.15		Routine. Maj MARTIN A.D.V.S. Cav. Corps. arrived to inspect unit but having received no orders	
"	18.5.15		nothing was ready. — A.D.V.S. gave orders to have everything ready for 10 a.m. 18.5.15.	
"	18.4.15	6 a.m.	Preparing for inspection by A.D.V.S.	
"	"	9.45 a.m.	Turned out for inspection	
"	"	10 a.m.	A.D.V.S. arrived & proceeded to make a very careful inspection of each man horse & equipment	

WAR DIARY or INTELLIGENCE SUMMARY.

(Erase heading not required.)

Army Form C. 2118.

No 20 Mob Vety Sec
8th Cav Bde

Instructions regarding War Diaries and Intelligence Summaries are contained in F. S. Regs., Part II. and the Staff Manual respectively. Title pages will be prepared in manuscript.

Place	Date	Hour	Summary of Events and Information	Remarks and references to Appendices
LA CARNOY	18.4.15		A.D.V.S. made few enquiries but suggested that 30 extra rations for the horses of the Section should always be carried — Quantity of spare shoes not quite up to War Establishment & other less important suggestions.	
		D.1230pm	Inspection over — Think men & horses satisfactory & afterwards General First Section was marked down as efficient.	
		12.30pm	Both sections recently refitted.	
	19.4.15		Routine.	
	20.4.15		Routine.	
	21.4.15		Routine — Evacuated 6 horses from STEENEBECQUE to NEUFCHATEL.	
	22.4.15		Routine.	
	23.4.15	9.50am	Received orders to move Section to Brigade rendezvous as SURCUS immediately on account of whole Brigade moving	
	25.4.15	10.30am	Moved off to SURCUS. & sent men to the headquarters of each unit to enquire number of horses & that would require evacuating in the event of Echelon B moving — Injured A.D. Staff of Echelon B would move more then & inform First Section had been warned for it to remain in billets ready to move at a moments notice	

1577 Wt. W10791/1773 500,000 1/15 D. D. & L. A.D.S.S./Forms/C. 2118.

WAR DIARY or INTELLIGENCE SUMMARY.

(Erase heading not required.)

Army Form C. 2118.

No. 20 Mob. Vety Sec.
8th Can. Div.

Instructions regarding War Diaries and Intelligence Summaries are contained in F. S. Regs., Part II. and the Staff Manual respectively. Title pages will be prepared in manuscript.

Place	Date	Hour	Summary of Events and Information	Remarks and references to Appendices
SURCUS	23.4.15	4 p.m.	Gave orders for section to return to billets & make arrangements for the collection of all sick horses next day.	JR
LA CARNOIS	24.4.15	8.0. a.m.	Took 36 horses & evacuated from STEENEBECQUE to NEUFCHATEL	
		2 p.m.	Received orders from AD.V.S. that no No. 13 & 14 M.V.S. have charge of men to collect sick to evacuate for the whole Division of Regiments ub HAZEBROUCK and might be billed upon to evacuate for the whole Division.	JR
		4 p.m.	Moved up to SURCUS also to be more central & referred to No. 13. M.V.S.	JR
SURCUS	25.4.15		Standing to- Exercise close to billets - Called in No. 13. M.V.S. & found that they had no news. Nor as I had, remounts having been disposed of.	JR
	26.4.15		Still standing to ready to move at a moment's notice - Exercise close to billets	JR
	27.4.15		Proceeded to sick horses from HAZEBROUCK to NEUFCHATEL	JR
	28.4.15	11 a.m.	Received orders to be ready to proceed up country to evacuate horses from regiments—	
		4 p.m.	Reinforcements received S.E. No. 3666 Sto. BROOMFIELD. Pte. Corporal P. Gaine A.V.S. called & left no note for billets.	JR
SURCUS	29.4.15	11 a.m.	Standing to waiting for orders to proceed up country. A.D.V.S. & AP.V.S. called with E.A.D.R. & inspected draught horses & limbers - much interested in anti-friction saddle made up by R's Cpl Gaine AVS. AD VS gave us orders to take whole section up country next day.	JR

1577 Wt. W10791/1773 500,000 1/15 D. D. & L. A.D.S.S./Forms/C. 2118.

WAR DIARY
or
INTELLIGENCE SUMMARY.
(Erase heading not required.)

No. 20 Mob: Vety Sn
8th Cav. Bde.

Army Form C. 2118.

Instructions regarding War Diaries and Intelligence Summaries are contained in F. S. Regs., Part II. and the Staff Manual respectively. Title pages will be prepared in manuscript.

Place	Date	Hour	Summary of Events and Information	Remarks and references to Appendices
SURCUS	30.4.15	8 a.m.	Left SURCUS to proceed to HdQrs of 8th Cav. Bde. not knowing where they were. Proceeded via HAZEBROUCK to STEENEVORDE - Made enquiries in HAZEBROUCK of anyone who the Brigade was but with no results - Saw Supply Officer who furnished the information required. Halted in field for water & feed then proceeded S of STEENEVORDE on HAZEBROUCK's STEENEVORDE road	Reff. M. at HAZEBROUCK 5A
		noon		
		2 p.m.	Arrived at the HdQs situated by the crossroads kilometre N.W. of ABEELE on the ABEELE - WATOU road - Section picketed in the open for the night in the same field as HdQ. - Visited regiments & collected horses	Bill. M. at HAZEBROUCK 5A
ABEELE	1.5.15	10 a.m.	Took section back to billets with HdQ of Essex B. at BLARING(HEM)	
		12 noon	Halter for watch as fast as sent full to get the interior ready	
BLARINGHEM		6 p.m.	Arrived in billets	

3rd Cavalry Division

20th Mtd Vety: Section

Vol III

187/56/0

WAR DIARY
or
INTELLIGENCE SUMMARY.
(Erase heading not required.)

Army Form C. 2118.

No 20 Mt. Vety Sec

Place	Date	Hour	Summary of Events and Information	Remarks and references to Appendices
ABEELE	1.5.15	10 a.m.	Left ABEELE with Section & four sick horses to return to billets at BLARINGHEM with Hd Qrs of Echelon B	
		12.30 h.	Halted for water & feed in some field on the outward journey.	
		1.51 p.m.	Started again for BLARINGHEM.	
BLARINGHEM		6 p.m.	Arrived in billets.	
BLARINGHEM	2.5.15		Routine work – Horses given only light exercise	
	3.5.15	9 a.m.	Received orders to report myself at Bde Hd Qrs next day 4.5.15. with pack of Section only –	
		4.30 p.m.	Left with 1 NCO & 8 men with one limbered wagon so as to arrive at Bde Hd Qs early next day. Have a complete day to collect horses if necessary. Left word with N.C.O. i/c of the rest of Section to collect horses & meet me that day at HAZEBROUCK to return from	
ABEELE	4.5.15	9.30 p.m.	Arrived at farm close to ABEELE & found 6 horses waiting for collection so billeted for the night in the farm.	
ABEELE	4.5.15	5 a.m.	Reveille – Made inquiries about the position of the Brigade but unable to find out anything about them until 9 a.m. when I saw a member of the Staff who gave me the necessary information	

WAR DIARY
or
INTELLIGENCE SUMMARY.

Army Form C. 2118.

No 20 Mb Vety Co

Place	Date	Hour	Summary of Events and Information	Remarks and references to Appendices
ABEELE	4.5.15	9 a.m.	Sent N.C.O. with three men to HAZEBROUCK with the sick horses already collected & proceeded with the rest of the section to B.Ed. Hd Qs at HOUTKERQUE.	
HOUTKERQUE	"	11 a.m.	Reported to Bde Hd Qs & visited regiments & on finding that they had no sick returned to HAZEBROUCK	
"	"	3 p.m.	Evacuated 19 horses & returned to Billets at BLARINGHEM	
BLARINGHEM	"	6 p.m.	Arrived in billets.	
"	5.5.15		Routine work	
"	6.5.15		Routine.	
"	7.5.15		Routine - Evacuated 14 sick horses - STEENEBECQUE to NEUFCHATEL	
"	"	6 p.m.	Moved to billets at LACARNOIS - Brigade returned to billets.	
LA CARNOIS	8.5.15		Routine.	
"	9.5.15	10 a.m.	Brigade ordered to move in motor busses leaving horses behind.	
"	"		Evacuated 18 horses - STEENEBECQUE to NEUFCHATEL	
"	10.5.15	-	Routine.	
"	11.5.15	-	Routine.	
"	12.5.15	-	Routine.	

WAR DIARY
or
INTELLIGENCE SUMMARY.
(Erase heading not required.)

No 20 Mob Vety Sec.

Army Form C. 2118.

Place	Date	Hour	Summary of Events and Information	Remarks and references to Appendices
L.A. CARNOIS	13.5.15	10 a.m.	Sent an N.C.O. to Advanced Vety Stores for drugs for the 15th Bde R.H.A.	
"	14.5.15		Routine	
"	15.5.15		Routine	
"	16.5.15		Routine	
"	17.5.15		Routine	
"	18.5.15		Evacuated 3 horses STEENEBECQUE to NEUFCHATEL	
"	19.5.15		Routine	
"	20.5.15		Routine	
"	21.5.15		Routine – Received orders to proceed to VLAMERTINGHE next day to collect 3 horses Rfn mk [signatures]	
"	22.5.15	2 p.m.	Left billets with one N.C.O. & four men to proceed to VLAMERTINGHE via HAZEBROUCK HAZEBROUCK SK	
			CAESTRE, BERTHEN, WESTOUTRE & RENINGHELST.	
VLAMERTINGHE	22.5.15	7 p.m.	Arrived VLAMERTINGHE collected horses & returned to REINGHELST for the night – Watered horses.	
RENINGHELST	22.5.15	10 p.m.	Billeted in a field for the night – Watered & fed – also night.	
"	23.5.15	5 a.m.	Reveille	
"	"	8 a.m.	Proceeded to Sth BERTHEN. FLETRE to a field North of PRADELLES	

Army Form C. 2118.

WAR DIARY
of
INTELLIGENCE SUMMARY. 20 Mobile Vety Section

(Erase heading not required.)

Instructions regarding War Diaries and Intelligence Summaries are contained in F. S. Regs., Part II. and the Staff Manual respectively. Title pages will be prepared in manuscript.

Place	Date	Hour	Summary of Events and Information	Remarks and references to Appendices
PRADELLES	23.5.15	12 noon	Off saddled watered & fed & rested for an hour.	
		1h.n	Resumed journey to billets at LA CARNOIS.	
LA CARNOIS		4 p.m	Arrived in billets.	
"	24.5.15		Routine. Maj. McINTYRE City J. McIntyre reported sick & sent away by 8th Cav. Fd. Ambulance.	OK
"	25.5.15		Routine. 22 horses evacuated to STEENEBECQUE & NEUFCHATEL	OK
"	26.5.15		Routine.	OK
"	27.5.15		Routine.	OK
"	28.5.15		Routine.	OK
"	29.5.15		Routine - Evacuated 26 horses STEENEBECQUE to NEUFCHATEL	OK
"	30.5.15		Routine. ROBINSON	OK
"	31.5.15		Routine. SE2754 Cpl L. A. Robinson reported arrived for duty from No9 Vety Hospital.	OK

3rd Cavalry Division

12/6341

20th Mortd Vety: Section

Vet IV

WAR DIARY
or
INTELLIGENCE SUMMARY.

Army Form C. 2118.

20 Mobile Vety Section

(Erase heading not required.)

Place	Date	Hour	Summary of Events and Information	Remarks and references to Appendices
A. CARNOY	1.6.15	—	Routine work.	
"	2.6.15		Routine work – Complaints from A.D.V.S. Cav. Corps. that this Division are evacuating too many horses & mules of all description to the other Divisions.	
"	3.6.15		Routine work.	
"	4.6.15		Conference at A.D.V.S. 3rd Cav. Div. Office to enquire into cause of evacuation of so many sick horses – Result- Horses evacuated as debility should have been removed cases in majority of cases – Yeomanry regiments evacuated more horses than the other regiments.	
			Evacuated 8 horses STEENBECQUE – NEUFCHATEL	
"	5.6.15	—	Routine work.	
"	6.6.15	—	Routine work	
"	7.6.15	—	Routine work	
"	8.6.15		Routine work	
"	9.6.15		Routine work	
"	10.6.15		Routine work. Horses cast by the G.O.C. taken over for evacuation.	
"	11.6.15		Evacuated 9 horses STEENBECQUE – NEUFCHATEL 20 horses cast by G.O.C. also evacuated.	
"	12.6.15		Routine – Received reinforcements 1 heavy draught horse & 1 Rider.	

WAR DIARY or INTELLIGENCE SUMMARY

Army Form C. 2118.

20 M'td Bde Vety Section

Place	Date	Hour	Summary of Events and Information	Remarks and references to Appendices
LA CARNOY	13.6.15		Routine work	
	14.6.15		Attended inspection by A.D.V.S. of Rgl.H horse Gde to X Royal Hussars - Inspection of	
	15.6.15		Ohin disease sent to 13th Mob Vety. Sec. from X Royal Hussars	
	16.6.15		Attended inspection by A.D.V.S. of horses of Essex Yeomanry, D & M Bde R.H.A. Valuators & horses STEENBECQUE & NEUFCHATEL	
	17.6.15		Routine	
	18.6.15		Routine	
	19.6.15		Routine	
	20.6.15		Routine	
	21.6.15		Routine	
	22.6.15		Evacuated 11 sick horses STEENEBECQUE — NEUFCHATEL	
	23.6.15		Routine	
	24.6.15		Routine	
	25.6.15		Routine	
	26.6.15		Routine	
	27.6.15		Routine	

WAR DIARY
or
INTELLIGENCE SUMMARY.

(Erase heading not required.)

Army Form C. 2118.

20 Mtr Vety Co

Place	Date	Hour	Summary of Events and Information	Remarks and references to Appendices
LA CAR NOIS.	28.6.15		Routine.	
	29.6.15		Routine.	
	30.6.15		Routine. Evacuated 13 horses STEENEBECQUE – NEUFCHATEL	

12/6341

3rd Cavalry Division

20th Mobile Vety Section

1st July 17

WAR DIARY
or
INTELLIGENCE SUMMARY.
(Erase heading not required.)

Army Form C. 2118.

2D Mtd. Bty. Section

Instructions regarding War Diaries and Intelligence Summaries are contained in F. S. Regs., Part II. and the Staff Manual respectively. Title pages will be prepared in manuscript.

Place	Date	Hour	Summary of Events and Information	Remarks and references to Appendices
LA CALNAU	1-7-15		Routine.	
	2-7-15		Routine	
	3-7-15		Routine	
	4-7-15		Routine	
	5-7-15		Routine	
	6-7-15		Routine	
	7-7-15		Routine	
	8-7-15		Routine – Roy Horse guards reported that a hare of flies has met with an increase. While swimming horses unable to walk down to their billets – Burned a plant after much difficulty & flies hove into the Section. Very fortunate in getting a plant as all certainly no this antidote is conveyed merely by small blows – if that had been one with the division it would have been more convenient.	
"	9-7-15		Routine.	
	10-7-15		Routine	
	11-7-15		Routine	
	12-7-15		Routine.	

WAR DIARY *20 Mobile Vety Section*
or
INTELLIGENCE SUMMARY.

Army Form C. 2118.

Instructions regarding War Diaries and Intelligence Summaries are contained in F. S. Regs., Part II. and the Staff Manual respectively. Title pages will be prepared in manuscript.

(Erase heading not required.)

Place	Date	Hour	Summary of Events and Information	Remarks and references to Appendices
LA CARNOY	13.7.15		Routine	
"	14.7.15		Routine	
"	15.7.15		Routine	
"	16.7.15		Routine. SE 4015 Pte Irving A.H. sent to Pte Chu S/A Ambulance Splittrinned	
			9 Sick horse evacuated STEENEBECQUE — NEUFCHATEL	
			SE 4690 O/RW Messer H SE 3869 Pte Smith SE 3920 Pte Wordo — sent to Pte Chu. S/A Ambulance	
"	17.7.15		— Returned with horses.	
"	18.7.15		Routine.	
"	19.7.15		Routine. No 4151 L/Sergt Parker R.E. reported himself for duty with this section from	
			No 14 Mob. Vety Sec.	
"	20.7.15		Routine.	
"	21.7.15		Routine. No 596 L/Cpl Neale reported himself for duty with this section from No 9 Vety Hospital.	
"	22.7.15		Routine. Crating by G.O.C. 3rd Can. Div.	
"	23.7.15		Routine. 20 Cast horses & 2 vety cases evacuated STEENEBECQUE — NEUFCHATEL	
			SE 4162 Pte Irving returned from hospital	
			SE 4433 Lt Col Williams A.V. Cps Section for duty with No 13 Vety Hospital	

WAR DIARY
or
INTELLIGENCE SUMMARY. 20 Mot. Vety. Sec.

Army Form C. 2118.

Place	Date	Hour	Summary of Events and Information	Remarks and references to Appendices
LA CARNOIS	24/7/15		342 L/Sgt Squires left return for duty at No 9 Vety hospital.	
	25/7/15		SE 3869 Pte Smith reported from hospital	
	26/7/15		Routine.	
	27/7/15		SE 4690 O/pl Moore A. & SE 3920 Pte Moore reported from hospital.	
	28/7/15		Routine.	
	29/7/15		Routine.	
	30/7/15		Routine.	

121/6983

3rd Cavalry Division

20th Mobile Vety: Section

Vol VI

August 15

WAR DIARY
or
INTELLIGENCE SUMMARY.
(Erase heading not required.)

Army Form C.2118

No. Mobile Veterinary Section

Place	Date	Hour	Summary of Events and Information	Remarks and references to Appendices
LA CARNOY	1.8.15		Routine. SE 1345 Pte Rutland & SE 319 Pte Runnigned for own Rouen	
"	2.8.15		Routine. 13 Mures evacuated STEENE BECQUE — NEUFCHATEL	
"	3.8.15		Routine.	
"	4.8.15		Routine. Evacuated 13 mures HAZEBROUCK — NEUFCHATEL.	
"	5.8.15		Routine.	
"	6.8.15		Moved to a new Brigade area — this section being billeted in PETIGNY.	
PETIGNY	7.8.15		Routine.	
"	8.8.15		Routine. SE 3310 Pte Anthony returned from own Rouen	
"	9.8.15		Routine.	
"	10.8.15		Routine.	
"	11.8.15		Routine.	
"	12.8.15		Routine.	
"	13.8.15		Routine.	
"	14.8.15		Routine. Evacuated 14 horses. ARQUES — NEUFCHATEL.	
"	15.8.15		Routine.	
"	16.8.15		Routine.	

WAR DIARY
or
INTELLIGENCE SUMMARY.

(Erase heading not required.)

Army Form C. 2118

Instructions regarding War Diaries and Intelligence Summaries are contained in F. S. Regs., Part II. and the Staff Manual respectively. Title pages will be prepared in manuscript.

Do Motor Veh Colm

Place	Date	Hour	Summary of Events and Information	Remarks and references to Appendices
PETIGNY	17.8.15		Routine	
"	18.8.15		Routine. SE 5477 Pte Cunliffe R.A. SE 3661 Pte Griffiths J. left section & join No 6 VCoy Arrived UK.	
"	19.8.15		Routine	
"	20.8.15		Routine.	
"	21.8.15		Routine.	
"	22.8.15		Routine	
"	23.8.15		Routine	
"	24.8.15		Routine	
"	25.8.15		Routine	
"	26.8.15		Routine. 16 Lorries convoyed ARQUES – NEUFCHATEL.	
"	27.8.15		Routine	
"	28.8.15		Routine. 371 Sergt Left. & 434 Sergt Faulkner arrived – 269 CSM Mansfield	
"			& 481 Pte Carter left section to join No 10 VCoy Arrived.	
"	29.8.15		Routine	
"	30.8.15		Routine.	
"	31.8.15		Routine – 11 Lorries convoyed ARQUES – NEUFCHATEL	

3rd Cavalry Division

121/6983

20th Mobile Vety. Sectn.

Vol VII
Sept 15

WAR DIARY 20 Militia V.Hty Section

INTELLIGENCE SUMMARY.

Army Form C. 2118

Place	Date	Hour	Summary of Events and Information	Remarks and references to Appendices
PETIGNY	1.9.15		Routine.	
	2.9.15		Routine.	
	3.9.15		Routine. Pte Fairman SE4449 recommended for duty as this Secn on account of ill health.	APR
	4.9.15		Routine.	
	5.9.15		Routine.	APR
	6.9.15		Routine.	APR
	7.9.15		Routine.	APR
	8.9.15		Routine.	APR
	9.9.15		Routine.	APR
	10.9.15		Routine Casting by G.O.C. 3rd Cav. Bn. (29 horses).	APR
	11.9.15		Evacuated horses shod by G.O.C ARQUES – NEUFCHATEL & also one other dicen case. (30 horses total)	APR
	12.9.15		Evacuated 37 sick horses. ARQUES – NEUFCHATEL– sesus ordered to join 39 Militia V.Hty Section.	APR

WAR DIARY or INTELLIGENCE SUMMARY

Army Form C. 2118

20 Mobile Vety Section

Place	Date	Hour	Summary of Events and Information	Remarks and references to Appendices
PETIGNY	12.9.15		Routine	
	14.9.15		Monthly kits Insp. inspection by O.C. 1st Bde. and Unesco property found with authorised his equipments sent from to Hayfield. — Each Pvs of the Unesco carried approximately 5 cwt.	
			Evacuated 10 horses ARQUES to NEUFCHATEL.	
	16.9.15		Routine. No 1 + 20 Sgt McMahon joined from No 13 Mobile Vety Section	
	17.9.15		Routine	
	18.9.15		Routine	
	19.9.15		Sick horses evacuated ARQUES to NEUFCHATEL — 434 Sgt Parchman to join No 13 Vety Hospital	
	20.9.15		Routine — Received orders to move with Ballon B to WESTREHEM	
	21.9.15		Evacuated 10 horses ARQUES — NEUFCHATEL. Moved section with Ballon B to WESTREHEM	
WESTREHEM	22.9.15		Standing to all day — Received orders for movement	
	28.9.15		Evacuated 15 horses ARQUES — NEUFCHATEL — Received orders to collect 6 horses left behind by the Kensington Yeomanry in FAUQUEMBERGUES and sent an N.C.O. to inspect them and see if they were fit to travel.	

1577 Wt.W10791/1773 500,000 1/15 D.D.&L. A.D.S.S./Forms/C. 2118.

Army Form C. 21[?]

WAR DIARY
or
INTELLIGENCE SUMMARY.
(Erase heading not required.)

Instructions regarding War Diaries and Intelligence Summaries are contained in F. S. Regs., Part II. and the Staff Manual respectively. Title pages will be prepared in manuscript.

of 20 Motor Vety Section

Place	Date	Hour	Summary of Events and Information	Remarks and references to Appendices
WESTREHEM	24.9.15		Collected the horses left behind by the Expeditionary Veterinary & inspected the horses of this Section B. Put in charge of Col. B of 13th Mobile Vety Sec.	
	25.9.15		Entrained 16 horses AIRE to ABBEVILLE granted return with Col. B to RINCQ — Billeted in field everybody sleeping out, very wet.	
	26.9.15		Stay at Billets & cleaned saddles etc — Inspected horses of Col. B — Capt Richardson AVC TF arrived with 2nd change of Col. B of 20th Mob Vety Sec & 13th Mob Vety Sec billets this Vety were of this no. of Col. B — Received orders from A.D.V.S. to take my Sec. A to join Col. A2 of the 5th Cav. Rly. next day	
	27.9.15 a.m		Lyft billets proceeded with 19 horses + 18 NCOs, orders to be London horses only with necessary transp. via AIRE - ST. HILAIRE - LILLERS - CHOQUES. LABUISSIERE to NOEUX LES MINES. Arrd by canal side but the S.O. of 5th Cav. Rly. who directed me to buy destination — hardly to find any one until we met the Supply Officer who could give us any idea where the Brigade was — Billeted in the open close to No 13 Mob Vety Section	
NOEUX LES MINES	28.9.15		Visited horses of the Brigade only found out some that would require	

1577 Wt. W10791/1773 500,000 1/15 D. D. & L. A.D.S.S/Forms/C. 2118.

Army Form C. 2118

WAR DIARY
20 Mobile Vety Sec.
or
INTELLIGENCE SUMMARY.
(Erase heading not required.)

Instructions regarding War Diaries and Intelligence Summaries are contained in F. S. Regs., Part II. and the Staff Manual respectively. Title pages will be prepared in manuscript.

Place	Date	Hour	Summary of Events and Information	Remarks and references to Appendices
NOEUX LES MINES.	26.9.15	4/0 a.m	marching — Moved section up with the rest of the Echelon A2. to the Brigade — Bivouac the horses collected in the morning.	
	29.9.15	8 a.m	Received an order that as the rear of the Brigade were moving at noon in rear to GOSNAY, proceed down on a flanged field opposite village.	
GOSNAY.	30.9.15	7 a.m	Visited units found that in the event of a sudden move should probably have enough & pleased to evacuate sick in the event of the Brigade remaining in present billets even if not more sufficiency shown to move with Brigade.	
		12.30 p.m	Received orders to furnish the A.F. o A2010 for A.B.u R.H.A. Ammunition Column "G" Batty R.H.A. & H.Q. 4th R.H.A. R.A.A.	
		2 p.m	Proceeded to look for the above units & make up for A A2010 AFA — took them personally to A.D.V.S 3rd Cav Div.	

121/7381

3rd Cavalry Division

20th British Vety: Section

Return

Oct 15

WAR DIARY or INTELLIGENCE SUMMARY.

Army Form C. 2118

20 Mobile Vety. Section

(Erase heading not required.)

Place	Date	Hour	Summary of Events and Information	Remarks and references to Appendices
GOSNAY	1/10/15	—	Remained in billets till 2.30.	
		2.30 p.m	Ordered to move by 2.30 p.m. to billets in LABEUVRIERE — visited regiments & collected 10 horses which were evacuated from NOEUX LES MINES to NEUFCHATEL	
		7.30 p.m	Arrived in billets in LABEUVRIERE	
LABEUVRIERE	2/10/15	—	Remained in billets — Inspected horses of "G" Battery.	
	3/10/15		Read that this Brigade would move during the day — units sent in three horses for evacuation —	
		11 a.m.	Received orders to move in rear of the Brigade. Moves the starting point at 12.15 p.m.	
		3 p.m.	arrived in billets at BURBURE.	
BURBURE	4/10/15		Section standing to all day — Visited 3rd Field Squadron R.E. & "G" Battery — Received two horses from the 10th Hussars	
BURBURE	5/10/15		Received 4 horses for evacuation — Evacuated 8 horses from LILLERS to NEUFCHATEL Visited "G" Battery, & 3rd Field Squadron.	
BURBURE	6/10/15		Routine work	
	7/10/15		Routine work	
	8/10/15		Routine work	

WAR DIARY or INTELLIGENCE SUMMARY

Army Form C. 2118

Do Notice Vety Belin

Place	Date	Hour	Summary of Events and Information	Remarks and references to Appendices
BURBURE	9.10.15		Routine.	JB
"	10.10.15		Receiving orders to hand over to Lieut Butcher. Moved to No 6 Vety. Hospital ROUEN. Evacuated 20 horses LILLERS — NEUFCHATEL. Inspected old shoe horses of O. Battery	JB
"	11.10.15		A.D.V.S. called & visited the G.O.C assigned to on his return gave no instructions not to move to ROUEN until I received further orders.	JB
"	12.10.15		LIEUT BUTCHER arriving Evacuated to take over charge of unit.	JB
"	13.10.15		Routine work — During over of station completed	JB
"	14.10.15		Routine work — Visited units.	JB
"	15.10.15		Routine S.E. 596 LP. Riffle left to join at Binsons Heim	JB
"	16.10.15		Routine — Visited A.D.V.S — Receiving orders to take over station — Completed	JB
"	17.10.15		Routine. Evacuated 8 No horses LILLERS — NEUFCHATEL	JB
"	18.10.15		Standing to all day expecting to move.	JB
"	"	7 p.m	Recv'd orders to move at 9 a.m 19.10.15.	JB
"	19.10.15	9 a.m	Rendezvous by CHURCH — Units to move individually	JB
RECLINGHEM	20.10.15	4 p.m	Arrived RECLINGHEM — Horses picketed in the open, men in barns. Stay of in billets expecting to move.	JB

WAR DIARY
or
INTELLIGENCE SUMMARY.   20 Mobile Vety Section.
(Erase heading not required.)

Army Form C. 2118

Place	Date	Hour	Summary of Events and Information	Remarks and references to Appendices
RECLINGHEM	21.10.18	9 a.m.	Moved to numerous billets in BEAUMETZ LES AIRE	
		12 noon	arrived in billets	
	22.10.18		Routine — Cleaned up billets	
	23.10.18		Routine — Cleaned up billets	
	24.10.18		Routine	
	25.10.18		Routine	
	26.10.18		Evacuated Horses AIRE – NEUFCHATEL	
			Routine — Visited units of Bde.	
	27.10.18		Routine — Visited units of Bde — Ollette 2 horses left behind by the Infantry NO AIRES	
	X.10.18		Routine — Visited units — S/Duprator Renaud reports himself for duty with 1	
	29.10.18		for Section	
			Routine.	
	30.10.18		Casting by G.O.C. 3 horses Cast & admitted into this Section for evacuation next day — Owing to the wet weather & the weakness of the litter the horses were continually breaking through & getting loose during the night.	

3rd Cavalry Division

20 Mos. Vet. Sec.
Nov. 1915
Vol. IX

121/7779

and

2W

WAR DIARY
of
INTELLIGENCE SUMMARY.

Army Form C. 2118

Instructions regarding War Diaries and Intelligence Summaries are contained in F. S. Regs., Part II. and the Staff Manual respectively. Title pages will be prepared in manuscript.

20 Mot. Vety Section.

Place	Date	Hour	Summary of Events and Information	Remarks and references to Appendices
BEAUMETZ LES AIRE	1-11-15	—	31 Cas horses evacuated AIRE – NEUFCHATEL	
"	2-11-15		6 Cas horses evacuated to the Remount Depot at GONNEHEM.	
"	3-11-15		Routine.	
"	4-11-15		Routine – 18 sick horses evacuated AIRE – NEUFCHATEL.	
"	5-11-15		Routine.	
"	6-11-15		Routine.	
"	7-11-15		Routine.	
"	8-11-15		Routine.	
"	9-11-15		Routine.	
"	10-11-15		14 sick horses & 1 Cas horse evacuated AIRE to NEUFCHATEL	
"	11-11-15		Routine	
"	12-11-15		Routine.	
"	13-11-15		Routine.	
"	14-11-15		Routine.	
"	15-11-15		Routine.	
"	16-11-15		Routine. 6 sick horses evacuated ; NEUFCHATEL	

Army Form C. 2118

WAR DIARY
or
INTELLIGENCE SUMMARY.

(Erase heading not required.)

20 Mob. Vety Sec.

Instructions regarding War Diaries and Intelligence Summaries are contained in F. S. Regs., Part II. and the Staff Manual respectively. Title pages will be prepared in manuscript.

Place	Date	Hour	Summary of Events and Information	Remarks and references to Appendices
BEAUMETZ LES AIRE - RIMBOVAL	17.11.15	8 a.m.	Moved off to new billets at RIMBOVAL via FRUGES.	
	"	2 p.m.	Arrived in new billets – Good shelter for horses & good sleeping accommodation for men –	
			Following N.C.O. & men reported for duty from No 13 Vety Hospital – 3103 L/c HARRIS	
			46464 L/Cpl LOFTHOUSE SE 4064 Pte BRYANT. SE 7877 Pte CLEGG. SE 2205 Pte SHEPHERD. SE 8286 Pte RYAN	
			SE 3647 Pte TALLANT. SE 5521 Pte TURNER.	
RIMBOVAL	18.11.15		Cleaned up billets. Following NCOs & men left for No 13 Vety Hospital. SE 420 Sergt	
			WOODHOUSE. SE 3754 C/S. ROBINSON. SE 4161 Pte ATKINSON. SE 3666 Pte BROOMFIELD. SE 3871 Pte DEAN	
			SE 3010 Pte HOLLOWAY. SE 3920 Pte WOODS.	
"	19.11.15		Routine	
"	20.11.15		Routine	
"	21.11.15		Routine	
"	22.11.15		Routine. SE 3866 Pte Deluce left to join No 13 Vety Hospital.	
"	23.11.15		Routine. 9 sick horses conducted to NEUFCHATEL from MARESQUEL	
"	24.11.15		Routine	
"	25.11.15		Routine	

Army Form C. 2118

WAR DIARY
or
INTELLIGENCE SUMMARY.
(Erase heading not required.)

20 Mot. V Coy N˚...

Instructions regarding War Diaries and Intelligence Summaries are contained in F. S. Regs., Part II. and the Staff Manual respectively. Title pages will be prepared in manuscript.

Place	Date	Hour	Summary of Events and Information	Remarks and references to Appendices
RIMBOVAL	26.11.15.		Routine	
	27.11.15		Routine	
	28.11.15		Routine	
	29.11.15		Routine	
	30.11.15		Sub Unros evacuated MARESQUEL — NEUFCHATEL.	

Dec - 1915.

20th Mobile Vet Section.

WAR DIARY
or
INTELLIGENCE SUMMARY.

Army Form C. 2118

20 Mob. Vety Sectur.

(Erase heading not required.)

Instructions regarding War Diaries and Intelligence Summaries are contained in F. S. Regs., Part II. and the Staff Manual respectively. Title pages will be prepared in manuscript.

Place	Date	Hour	Summary of Events and Information	Remarks and references to Appendices
RIMBOVAL	1.12.15		Sick horses evacuated MARESQUEL – NEUFCHATEL	
"	2.12.15		Routine	OBE
"	3.12.15		Routine	OBE
"	4.12.15		Routine	OBE
"	5.12.15		Routine	OBE
"	6.12.15		Routine. SE 2980 Pte Oreo & SE 4469 Pte Buchanan arrived for duty from No 3 Vety Hospital	OBE
"	7.12.15		Routine	OBE
"	8.12.15		Routine	OBE
"	9.12.15		Routine	OBE
"	10.12.15		Routine	OBE
"	11.12.15		Routine	OBE
"	12.12.15		Routine	OBE
"	13.12.15		Routine	OBE
"	14.12.15		Routine	OBE
"	15.12.15		Routine	OBE
"	16.12.15		Routine	OBE

Army Form C. 2118.

WAR DIARY
or
INTELLIGENCE SUMMARY.   30 Mtr. Vety Section

(Erase heading not required.)

Instructions regarding War Diaries and Intelligence Summaries are contained in F. S. Regs., Part II. and the Staff Manual respectively. Title pages will be prepared in manuscript.

Place	Date	Hour	Summary of Events and Information	Remarks and references to Appendices
DOMBOVAL	17.12.15		Routine.	
"	18.12.15		Inoculated 292 horses of "G" Batty – others influenal too.	
"	19.12.15		Inoculated 631 horses of the Essex Yeomanry	
"	20.12.15		Inoculated horses of the Royal Horse Guards.	
"	21.12.15		Evacuated 18 horses to NEUFCHATEL	
"	22.12.15		Inoculated horses of 10th Roy Hussars.	
"	23.12.15		Inoculated horses of the Brigade Headquarters	
"	24.12.15		Inoculated 29 horses of the 8th Cav Field Ambulance.	
"	25.12.15		Christmas Day 1 M HR no a Sunday	
"	26.12.15		Routine.	
"	27.12.15		Routine.	
"	28.12.15		Routine	
"	29.12.15		Routine	
"	30.12.15		Routine	
"	31.12.15		Routine	

WAR DIARY
or
INTELLIGENCE SUMMARY. No. Mobile Vety Sec.
(Erase heading not required.)

Army Form C. 2118.

Place	Date	Hour	Summary of Events and Information	Remarks and references to Appendices
RIMBOVAL	1.1.16	—	Routine	ABM
"	2.1.16	—	Routine	ABM
"	3.1.16		Evacuated 11 horses – MONTREUIL – NEUFCHATEL	ABM
	4.1.16		Routine	ABM
	5.1.16		Routine	ABM
	6.1.16		Routine	ABM
	7.1.16		Routine	ABM
	8.1.16		Routine	ABM
	9.1.16		Routine	ABM
	10.1.16		Evacuated 7 horses MONTREUIL – NEUFCHATEL –	ABM
	11.1.16		Routine	ABM
	12.1.16		Routine	ABM
	13.1.16		Routine	ABM
	14.1.16		SE 3117 Pte LEWIS Attached to Gm 3rd Mammoth Brigade as a veterinary orderly	ABM
	15.1.16		Routine	ABM

WAR DIARY
or
INTELLIGENCE SUMMARY.   20 Mobile Vety Section.

(Erase heading not required.)

Army Form C. 2118.

Instructions regarding War Diaries and Intelligence Summaries are contained in F. S. Regs., Part II. and the Staff Manual respectively. Title pages will be prepared in manuscript.

Place	Date	Hour	Summary of Events and Information	Remarks and references to Appendices
RIMBOVAL	16.1.16		Routine.	
"	17.1.16		Evacuated 4 horses MONTREVIL – NEUFCHATEL	[initials]
"	18.1.16		Routine.	[initials]
"	19.1.16		Routine.	[initials]
"	20.1.16		Routine.	[initials]
"	21.1.16		Routine.	[initials]
"	22.1.16		Routine.	[initials]
"	23.1.16		Routine.	[initials]
"	24.1.16		Evacuated 5 horses MONTREVIL – NEUFCHATEL	[initials]
"	25.1.16		Routine.	[initials]
"	26.1.16		Evacuated 24 cases horses MONTREVIL – NEUFCHATEL	[initials]
"	28.1.16		Routine.	[initials]
"	29.1.16		Routine.	[initials]
"	30.1.16		Routine.	[initials]
"	31.1.16		Evacuated 9 cases horses & 23 sick horses MONTREVIL – NEUFCHATEL	[initials]

Army Form C. 2118.

WAR DIARY
or
INTELLIGENCE SUMMARY.   No. 20 Mob. Vety Section
(Erase heading not required.)

Instructions regarding War Diaries and Intelligence Summaries are contained in F. S. Regs., Part II. and the Staff Manual respectively. Title pages will be prepared in manuscript.

Place	Date	Hour	Summary of Events and Information	Remarks and references to Appendices
RIMBOVAL	1.2.16		Routine.	
	2.2.16		Routine.	
	3.2.16		Routine.	
	4.2.16		Routine.	
	5.2.16		Routine.	
	6.2.16		Routine.	
	7.2.16		Routine.	
	8.2.16		Routine.	
	9.2.16		Routine — Evacuated 9 skin disease cases NEUFCHATEL	
	10.2.16		Routine.	
	11.2.16		Routine.	
	12.2.16		Routine.	
	13.2.16		Routine.	
	14.2.16		Evacuated 10 sick horses to NEUFCHATEL.	
	15.2.16		Routine.	
	16.2.16		Routine.	

WAR DIARY
or
INTELLIGENCE SUMMARY.

(Erase heading not required.)

Army Form C. 2118.

No. 20 Mob. Vety Section

Place	Date	Hour	Summary of Events and Information	Remarks and references to Appendices
RIMBOVAL	17.2.16		Routine.	
	18.2.16		Routine.	
	19.2.16		Routine.	
	20.2.16		Routine.	
	21.2.16		10 sick horses evacuated to NEUFCHATEL.	
	22.2.16		Routine.	
	23.2.16		Routine.	
	24.2.16		Routine.	
	25.2.16		Routine.	
	26.2.16		Routine.	
	27.2.16		Routine.	
	28.2.16		Routine.	
	29.2.16		Routine.	

WAR DIARY or INTELLIGENCE SUMMARY.

Army Form C. 2118.

No. 20 Mobile Vety. Section

Place	Date	Hour	Summary of Events and Information	Remarks and references to Appendices
RIMBOVAL	1.3.16		Routine	
"	2.3.16		Routine	
"	3.3.16		Routine	
"	4.3.16		Routine	
"	5.3.16		Routine	
"	6.3.16		Two sick animals evacuated to NEUFCHATEL – 8 sick horses also evacuated	
"	7.3.16		Routine	
"	8.3.16		Routine	
"	9.3.16		Routine	
"	10.3.16		Routine	
"	11.3.16		Routine	
"	12.3.16		Routine	
"	13.3.16		Routine. 6 sick horses evacuated to NEUFCHATEL	
"	14.3.16		Routine	
"	15.3.16		Routine	
"	16.3.16		Routine	

WAR DIARY
or
INTELLIGENCE SUMMARY. No Mobile Vety Section

Army Form C. 2118.

(Erase heading not required.)

Instructions regarding War Diaries and Intelligence Summaries are contained in F.S. Regs., Part II. and the Staff Manual respectively. Title pages will be prepared in manuscript.

Place	Date	Hour	Summary of Events and Information	Remarks and references to Appendices
RIA BOYAL	17.3.16		8 sick horses evacuated to NEUFCHATEL. Routine.	
	18.3.16		Routine.	
	19.3.16		Routine	
	20.3.16		7 sick horses evacuated to N° E OF CHATEL	
	21.3.16		Routine	
	22.3.16		Routine.	
	23.3.16		Routine.	
	24.3.16		Routine.	
	25.3.16		Routine — On light draught remount joined.	
	26.3.16		Routine.	
	27.3.16		10 sick horses evacuated to NEUFCHATEL.	
	28.3.16		Routine.	
	29.3.16		Sick men transferred to 1st Labour Batt. R.E. FRUGES.	
	30.3.16		Routine.	
	31.3.16		Routine.	

Army Form C. 2118.

WAR DIARY
or
INTELLIGENCE SUMMARY. 20 Mitra Vety Section.
(Erase heading not required.)

Instructions regarding War Diaries and Intelligence Summaries are contained in F. S. Regs., Part II. and the Staff Manual respectively. Title pages will be prepared in manuscript.

Place	Date	Hour	Summary of Events and Information	Remarks and references to Appendices
RIMBOVAL	1-4-16		Routine	
	2-4-16		Routine	
	3-4-16		14 horses evacuated NEUFCHATEL	
	4-4-16		Routine	
	5-4-16		Routine	
	6-4-16		Routine	
	7-4-16		Routine	
	8-4-16		Routine	
	9-4-16		Routine	
	10-4-16		11 horses evacuated NEUFCHATEL	
	11-4-16		Routine	
	12-4-16		Routine	
	13-4-16		Routine	
	14-4-16		32 Cases horses evacuated to ABBEVILLE. 7. dis horses evacuated ABBEVILLE	
	15-4-16		Routine	
	16-4-16		Routine	

1577 Wt. W10791/1773 500,000 1/15 D. D. & L. A.D.S.S./Forms/C. 2118.

Army Form C. 2118.

WAR DIARY
or
INTELLIGENCE SUMMARY. 20 Mobile Vety Section

(Erase heading not required.)

Place	Date	Hour	Summary of Events and Information	Remarks and references to Appendices
RIMBOVAL	14.4.16		7 Sick horses evacuated to ABBEVILLE.	
"	16.4.16		Routine.	
"	19.4.16		Routine.	
"	20.4.16		Routine.	
"	21.4.16		Routine.	
"	22.4.16		Routine.	
"	23.4.16		Routine.	
"	24.4.16		13. Sick & 3 Cases horses evacuated to ABBEVILLE.	
"	25.4.16		Routine.	
"	25.4.16		Routine.	
"	26.4.16		Routine.	
"	27.4.16		25 Cases horses & 3 sick horses evacuated to ABBEVILLE.	
"	28.4.16		Routine.	
"	29.4.16		Routine.	
"	30.4.16		Routine.	

Instructions regarding War Diaries and Intelligence Summaries are contained in F. S. Regs., Part II. and the Staff Manual respectively. Title pages will be prepared in manuscript.

Army Form C. 2118.

WAR DIARY
or
INTELLIGENCE SUMMARY. 20 Mobile Vety Section

(Erase heading not required.)

Vol 15

Instructions regarding War Diaries and Intelligence Summaries are contained in F. S. Regs., Part II. and the Staff Manual respectively. Title pages will be prepared in manuscript.

Place	Date	Hour	Summary of Events and Information	Remarks and references to Appendices
RIMBOVAL	1.5.16		20 sick horses evacuated to NEUFCHATEL.	
"	2.5.16		Routine	
"	3.5.16		Routine	
"	4.5.16		Routine	
"	5.5.16		Routine	
"	6.5.16		Routine	
"	7.5.16		Routine	
"	8.5.16		9 Cart horses + 2 sick horses evacuated to ABBEVILLE.	
"	9.5.16		Routine. SE/A375 – Private HAYNES evacuated sick to Divisional Rest Station.	
"	10.5.16		Private HAYNES evacuated to L of C.	
"	11.5.16		Routine – Evacuated 19 cart horses & 4 sick horses to ABBEVILLE – Received orders that this section would remain in billets whilst the 3rd Cav. Div. was away in the manoeuvre area around ABBEVILLE & would take over the sick horses of the whole division for evacuation prior to that departure of the Division.	APP. A.
"	12.5.16		Received horses of the 7th Cav. Reg.	
"	13.5.16		Received horses of the 6th & 8th Cav. Regs.	

WAR DIARY or INTELLIGENCE SUMMARY

Army Form C. 2118.

30 Mtd. Vety. Sections

Place	Date	Hour	Summary of Events and Information	Remarks and references to Appendices
RIMBOVAL	4.5.16	—	Evacuated 35 sick horses to NEUFCHATEL.	JB
"	15.5.16	6 a.m.	The 8th Cav. Bde. with the exception of details of 8th Cav. Fd. Amb., details of two regiments & the whole of the 30 Mtd. Vety. Sec. I left for the manoeuvre area.	JB
"	16.5.16		Routine.	JB
"	17.5.16		Routine.	JB
"	18.5.16		Routine.	JB
"	19.5.16		Routine.	JB
"	20.5.16		Routine.	JB
"	21.5.16		Routine. Evacuated 8 sick horses to NEUFCHATEL – Brigade returned to billets.	JB
"	22.5.16		Routine.	JB
"	23.5.16		Routine.	JB
"	24.5.16		Routine. Eleven sick horses evacuated to NEUFCHATEL.	JB
"	25.5.16		Routine.	JB
"	26.5.16		Routine.	JB
"	27.5.16		Routine.	JB
"	28.5.16		16 horses evacuated to NEUFCHATEL. S/4988 Pte BROWN reported his arrival for duty as a Clerk from No 2 Vety Hospital	JB

Army Form C. 2118.

WAR DIARY
or
INTELLIGENCE SUMMARY. 20th Mr. V Hyde

(Erase heading not required.)

Place	Date	Hour	Summary of Events and Information	Remarks and references to Appendices
RIMBOVAL	29.5.16		Received notice that the Brigade would move to MERLIMONT on 31.5.16.	
"	30.5.16		Routine – Pte Smith SIGLEY (SE 4649) reported for duty from No 7 Vety Hospital	
		2 P.m.	Issued kits to the men & picketed wagons.	
"	31.5.16	8.30 am	Section paraded in full marching order.	
		9.2 am	Section moved off via via the 8th Cav Fd. Ambulance – Ross Yeomanry Ambulance – Route – EMBRY – BOUGERS – HESMOND – BEAUVRAINVILLE – BRIMEUX – BEAUMERIE ST MARTIN – ECUIRES – SORRUS – ST AUBIN – MERLIMONT.	
LOISON BRIMEUX		10.30 am	Watered in a running stream at LOISON.	
		12.15 pm	Off saddled – watered & fed	
		1.15 pm	Saddled up & moved off.	
MERLIMONT		4 pm	Arrived at destination – horses picketed in a field – men in bivouac	
			One Corporal & 2 men left behind in charge of 6 sick horses.	

Appendix A.

3 C D 4275.

S.G. 1563.

8th Cavalry Brigade.

In view of the move of the Division to the Training Area the following Veterinary arrangements will be made :-

No 14 Mobile Veterinary Section to evacuate all sick to No 20 Mobile Veterinary Section on or before 12th May.

No 13 Mobile Veterinary Section to evacuate all sick to No 20 Mobile Veterinary Section on or before 14th May.

Nos 13 & 14 Mobile Veterinary Sections will move under Brigade arrangements, reporting to Divisional Headquarters each evening by wire where their position is and the number of casualties received.

The sick of the 8th Cavalry Brigade will be dealt with by nearest Mobile Veterinary Section.

Sick will be evacuated to No 22 Veterinary Hospital at ABBEVILLE.

H.Q. 3 C D.
11th May 1918.

(Sgd) W.P.Cosens, Major, for
Lieut-Colonel.
A.A.& Q.M.G., 3rd Cavalry Division.

2.

Officer Commanding,
  Royal Horse Guards.   "C" Battery. R.H.A.
  Tenth Royal Hussars.   8th Cav Fld Ambce.
  Essex Yeomanry.   8th Machine Gun Sqdn.
                             20th Mobile Veterinary Section.

For information and guidance.

11/5/18.

Captain,
Staff Captain, 8th Cavalry Bde.

20 Bob. V8y Section. Army Form C. 2118. 3c

WAR DIARY or INTELLIGENCE SUMMARY.

Vol 16

Place	Date	Hour	Summary of Events and Information	Remarks and references to Appendices
MERLIMONT	1.6.16		Routine	
"	2.6.16		Routine. Bull on the same	
"	3.6.16		16 horses evacuated to Neufchatel by rail.	
"	4.6.16		Routine - Summary. Horses on the sick - Bull on the same	
"	5.6.16		Routine	
"	6.6.16		Routine	
"	7.6.16		Routine	
"	8.6.16		19 horses evacuated to Neufchatel by rail	
"	9.6.16		2 horses skin disease) evacuated to Neufchatel by road.	
"	10.6.16	8 a.m.	Left Merlimont to return to permanent billets at Rimboval - Route. St Aubin Sorrus Ecoires Brimeux Aix en Issart Sempy Henoville Rimboval	
		12 noon	Watered & fed at Brimeux.	
		2.30 p.m.	Arrived Rimboval.	
RIMBOVAL	11.6.16		Routine. Se 4968 Pte Brown evacuated to Base sick.	
"	12.6.16		Routine.	
"	13.6.16		Evacuated 10 horses Beaurainville Neufchatel	

WAR DIARY or INTELLIGENCE SUMMARY.

Army Form C. 2118.

20 Mob. Vety Section.

(Erase heading not required.)

Instructions regarding War Diaries and Intelligence Summaries are contained in F. S. Regs., Part II. and the Staff Manual respectively. Title pages will be prepared in manuscript.

Place	Date	Hour	Summary of Events and Information	Remarks and references to Appendices
RIMBOVAL	14.6.16		Routine	
"	15.6.16		Routine	
"	16.6.16		Routine	
"	17.6.16		Routine — Received news that we should probably move on 24.6.16	
"	18.6.16		Routine. 36 sick horses evacuated to NEUFCHATEL	
"	19.6.16		Routine	
"	20.6.16		Routine	
"	21.6.16		Evacuated 10 sick horses to NEUFCHATEL	
"	22.6.16		6 sick horses evacuated NEUFCHATEL	
"	23.6.16		Routine — Received orders for move	
"	24.6.16		9 horses evacuated to 13 Mob. Vety Sec — Section packing up ready to move	
		5 p.m.	at night. SE 3606 Pte Phillips admitted to Hospital	×A.M.A.
		6:30 p.m.	Section turned in full marching order moved off in rear of His 6th Div. Sn. Amb. to starting point to arrived ×	
		8:30 p.m.	At starting point	
		10 p.m.	Section moves off in rear of Echelon A	

WAR DIARY
or
INTELLIGENCE SUMMARY.

(Erase heading not required.)

20 Bat. Vty Co.

Army Form C. 2118.

Instructions regarding War Diaries and Intelligence Summaries are contained in F. S. Regs., Part II. and the Staff Manual respectively. Title pages will be prepared in manuscript.

Place	Date	Hour	Summary of Events and Information	Remarks and references to Appendices
REGNIERE ECLUSE	25.6.16	3.30a	Arrived at temporary billets. — Night fine but very dark —	
		10 a	Received orders for the next move	APP. B
			All horses standing in steam. Dried their legs.	
		6.30p	Saddled up ready to move off in rear of 8th Cav. Div. & not to starting point.	
		8.30p	As starting point — troubles in rear of Echelon proceed on rear Echelon A but left the two wagons on rear of Echelon B	
			Long trek with slight interruptions — night very dark but fine	
ROUEN	26.6.16	2 am	Arrived at destination	
			On examination I.to transport found that the axle of the rear half of an officers limber had cracked on tow — having Hopp'd Platoon just along it	
			by an A.S. Corps workshop — wagon for western half limber	
		2 am	Received orders for tonights move —	x APP. C
		8 pm	Saddled up & waited for regiments. Two starting points as our billets were close by.	
		9 pm	Moved off in a downpour of rain which lasted all night — left standard road horse lines. Echelon B proceeded with rest of section behind Echelon A	

WAR DIARY
or
INTELLIGENCE SUMMARY.

20th M.V. Vety Section

Army Form C. 2118.

(Erase heading not required.)

Place	Date	Hour	Summary of Events and Information	Remarks and references to Appendices
BONNAY	27.6.16	a.m.	Arrived at Place of concentration - Ruboton where there are no of exits - Field practically under water two men had a tree to sleep in.	
"	28.6.16		All the horses of the Section arrived during night + fut- sun very little to was of night. Section served saddlery - kit. Evacuated 3 horses to 14 Mob. Vety Section.	
"	29.6.16		Routine. Received men - from M.D.V.S. of 3rd Cav. Div. relieving to the position of	
"	30.6.16		Instructions the Section in the event of a move forward - 13 o 14 M.B. Vety Sec. would collect the horses from this section Evacuees to No 6 N4 were to take them to Rubehead.	
"			Routine. Received Orders for evacuation from the whole terrain. Received orders to have everything packed by 6:30 a.m. 1.7.16 & stand to ready to move us to horses rations.	

APP. A
Secret

[Stamp: H.Q. 8th CAVALRY BRIGADE / B.M. 714/5 / 3rd CAVALRY DIVISION]

Officer Commanding.
- Royal Horse Guards.
- 10th. Royal Hussars.
- Essex Yeomanry.
- 8th. Machine Gun Squadron.
- 'G' Battery, R.H.A.
- 8th. C.F.A.
- 20th. M.V.S.
- Staff Captain, 8th. Cav. Bde.
- Transport Officer, "
- A.D.C. "
- Supply and Requisitioning Officer, 8th. Cav. Bde.
- 2/Lt. HANN Royal Horse Guards.

---

1. The Brigade moves into new (temporary area) on the night 24th./25th. inst.

2. (a) **Brigade Starting Point.** — Cross Roads just W. of 1st. L. of LE BUT de MARLES. Time 8.20 p.m.

   (b) **Route from Starting Point** — ST. REMY AUX BOIS – SAULCHOY – ARGOULES to temporary area. (see para. 6).

   (c) **Order of March.** —
   Headquarters, 8th. Cav. Bde.
   Royal Horse Guards.
   8th. Machine Gun Squadron.
   10th. Royal Hussars.
   Essex Yeomanry.   *
   'G' Battery, R.H.A.   *
   8th. C.F.A.   *
   'A' Echelon.
   20th. M.V.S.   *
   'B' Echelon.

3. Rendez-vous at Starting Point as under –
   Royal Horse Guards. Head 50 yards short of Starting Point, tail towards MARANT.
   8th. Machine Gun Squadron behind Royal Horse Guards.
   10th. Royal Hussars behind Machine Gun Squadron, head of 10th. to halt just short of MARANT till M.G.Sqdn. is clear.
   Essex Yeomanry. Head 50 yards short of Starting Point, tail towards MARENLA.
   'G' Battery Behind Essex Yeomanry.
   8th. C.F.A. Behind 'G' Battery.
   20th. M.V.S. Behind 8th. C.F.A.

4. 'A' and 'B' Echelon march to Starting Point in rear of Units.
   Each Unit on passing Starting Point will hand over its 'A' Echelon to 2/Lt. HANN, Royal Horse Guards, 'B' Echelon to Captain BAKER.

5. Units will send a representative to report at Starting Point as soon as they are closed up and ready to march.

6. Billetting areas are –
Bde. H.Q., Sigs. 8th. C.F.A. 20th. M.V.S.	REGNIERE-ECLUSE.
'G' Battery and E.Y.	VIRONCHAUX.
10th. Hussars.	MACHY.
R.H.Guards.	BERNAY.
M.G.Sqdn.	La BOCAILLE.

23/6/16.

Sd. S.J. HARDY. Capt,
Brigade Major, 8th. Cavalry Brigade.

NOTES.
(1). The Starting Point of 9th. Cav. Bde. is AUBIN-ST-VAAST, at 8.39 p.m., and their tail has to be clear of BEAURAINVILLE by 8.50 p.m.

Notes (contd).

2. # The 7th. Cavalry Brigade march to their Starting Point
(BEAURAINVILLE) via HENOVILLE and EMBRY, to arrive at
Starting Point by 8.30 p.m.

   Essex Tail must be clear of BOUBERS by 6.45 p.m.
   'G' Battery   "   "   "   7.   p.m.
   C.F.A.   "   "   "   7.15 p.m.
   all above marching to Brigade Starting Point via ST& DENOUEX
   and MARENLA.

3.   Tail of Brigade must be S. of River AUTHIE by 12 mid-night.

APP B

Distribution as B.M. 714/3.

            to-night
1. Brigade will continue its march/25th./26th. to new area. The move will completed by 3 a.m. 26th.

2. (a) Brigade Starting Point forked Roads just N. of Second C of CRECY. Time 8.30 p.m.

  (b) Route from Brigade Starting Point — DOMVAST — ST. RIQUIER — AILLY — MOUFLERS — FLIXECOURT.

  (c) Order of March. (following 7th. Cavalry Brigade).
    Headquarters.
    Essex Yeomanry.
    10th. Hussars.
    Royal Horse Guards.
    Machine Gun Squadron.
    'G' Battery. R.H.A.
    8th. C.F.A.
    'A' Echelon.
    20th. M.V.S.
    'B' Echelon.

  (d) 'A' and 'B' Echelons (order of march as above) will be handed over as usual as Units pass Starting Point.

3. Units rendez-vous as follows —
Essex Yeomanry	Head 50 yards short of Starting Point tail towards VIRONCHAUX.
10th. Hussars	Head 50 yards short of Starting Point tail towards MACHIEL.
Royal Horse Guards	Behind 10th. Hussars.
8th. M.G.Sqdn	Behind Royal Horse Guards.
'G' Battery	Behind 8th. M.G.Sqdn.
8th. C.F.A.	Behind 'G' Battery.
20th. M.V.S.	Behind 8th. C.F.A.

N.B. 7th. Brigade must be allowed to clear MACHIEL before going through it.

4. New area ST. OUEN — BETHENCOURT ST. OUEN. Allottment separately

             Sd. S.J.HARDY, Captain,
25/8/16.   Brigade Major, 8th. Cavalry Brigade.

BM Y/4/6.

On tonight march we reach camp via Road from LA NEUVILLE through △ of BONNAY.

No troops or either batchelons may go by the more westerly road or approach the camp by BONNAY village itself.

The easterly road from LA NEUVILLE which is merely marked as a track on the 1/100-000 map is passable for all traffic.

(sd) G Hardy Capt.
B.M. 8ᵗʰ Bde.

APPC.   BM 714/5.

1. Brigade will continue its march to-night 26/27th. to the CORBIE area.
Move to be completed by 3 am. 27th.

2.(a) Route — ST. VAAST en CHAUSSÉE — AMIENS CITADEL — DAOURS — LANEUVILLE — BONNAY.

(b) Order of march — H. Qrs., 10th Hrs., RHGds, Essex Yeo, M.G. Sqdn., G Battery, 8th 6. F.A.; A Echelon; 20th M.V.S.; B Echelon.

3.(a) Head of 10th Hussars will pass cross Roads at S.E. exit of ST. OUEN on the ST. VAAST en CHAUSSÉE road at 8. p.m.
RHGds. will follow 10th Hussars' tail as it clears above mentioned cross Roads.
Essex and M.G. Sqdn. follow RHGds
'G' Battery follow tail of M.G. Sqdn. as it clears cross Roads (above).
6.F.A. M.V.S. follow tail of G Battery as it clears cross Roads (above).

(b)

(b) 'A' and 'B' echelons will be handed over as usual as Units pass the 5 Road Junction 800 yards N. of DE of FORET DE VIGNACOURT.

(c) Units must make a liason with unit preceding them in order of march, so that they fall into their proper place in the column.

4 (a) New area is just E of the Y of BONNAY

(b) Guides meet units at X rds of LA NEUVILLE.

5, Attention must be paid to concealment by day. Horses must be picqueted in small groups under cover of trees when available.

26/6/16.   Brigade Major, 8 Can. Bde
            Captain

WAR DIARY or **INTELLIGENCE SUMMARY.**   Army Form C. 2118.

20 Mob Vety Section

Place	Date	Hour	Summary of Events and Information	Remarks and references to Appendices
BONNAY	1.7.16		Standing to with everything packed awaiting orders - Evacuated 28 sick horses to MERICOURT station they were taken over by N.C.O's sent from No.7 Vety Hospital attached to No. 12 Mobile Vety Section. No more took place and in the evening April of preparations were relaxed	
"	2.7.16		Standing to until evening.	
"	3.7.16		Routine work - Received orders that Brigade would move to the ABBEVILLE area the following day - Collected all horses for evacuation from the Division -	
"	4.7.16 4.50am	Sent off Sergts. men off to new billeting area - Evacuated 9 sick horses to MERICOURT and followed the Brigade via DAOURS, AMIENS, AILLY SUR SOMME, PONT REMY to Billets at BAILLEUL	
BAILLEUL	5.7.16		Routine work	
"	6.7.16		Routine	
"	7.7.16		Routine - Evacuated 21 sick horses by road to No.22 Vety Hospital - Ordered to be ready to move at 5 hours notice.	
"	8.7.16		Move to be ready to move at 1½ hours notice - Evacuated 1 sick horse to No.22 Vety Hospital and took men into ABBEVILLE to be exchanged	

Vol 17 3e

WAR DIARY or INTELLIGENCE SUMMARY.

Army Form C. 2118.

30 Mobile Vety Section

Place	Date	Hour	Summary of Events and Information	Remarks and references to Appendices
BAILLEUL	8.7.16	1 a.m.	Brigade orders to turn out at one relation to the neighbourhood of BONNAY i.e. CORBIE area – Unable to start with the Section as the lorries had not returned from ABBEVILLE	
		5 p.m.	Move off via PONTREMY, PICQUIGNY, AILLY SUR SOMME, AMIENS, VECQUEMONT to CORBIE – Bivouaced in field with whole Division	
CORBIE BONNAY	9.7.16	4 h.m.	Moved to BONNAY SE 16/66 Pte McGUIGAN reported for duty from No 4 Vety Hospital	
"	10.7.16		Routine	
"	11.7.16		Evacuated 18 sick horses to MERICOURT	
"	12.7.16		Routine	
"	13.7.16		Routine. Sick horses evacuated to MERICOURT	
"	14.7.16		Routine	
"	15.7.16		Routine. 4 horses evacuated to MERICOURT	
"	16.7.16		Routine	
"	17.7.16		Routine	
"	18.7.16		24 horses evacuated to MERICOURT	
"	19.7.16		Routine	

WAR DIARY
or
INTELLIGENCE SUMMARY.

(Erase heading not required.)

Army Form C. 2118.

20 Mot. Vety. Sec

Instructions regarding War Diaries and Intelligence Summaries are contained in F. S. Regs., Part II. and the Staff Manual respectively. Title pages will be prepared in manuscript.

Place	Date	Hour	Summary of Events and Information	Remarks and references to Appendices
BONNAY	20.7.16		6 horses evacuated to MERICOURT	
	21.7.16		Routine.	
	22.7.16		Routine	
	23.7.16		Routine. 10 sick horses evacuated to MERICOURT	
	24.7.16		SE/88 Pte MARSHALL reported his arrival for duty from No.1 Convalescent Horse Depot	
	25.7.16		9 sick horses evacuated to MERICOURT.	
	26.7.16		6 horses evacuated to MERICOURT.	
	27.7.16		Routine.	
	28.7.16		Routine. 2 sick horses evacuated to 13 Mot Vety. Sec	
	29.7.16		22 sick horses evacuated to MERICOURT.	
	30.7.16		Routine.	
	31.7.16		Routine - Received orders that we should move materials next day.	
			SE/6160 Pte McGUIGAN rear guard No 2 Vety Hospital.	

Army Form C. 2118.

WAR DIARY
or
INTELLIGENCE SUMMARY.   20 Mobile Vety Sectin.

(Erase heading not required.)

Vol 18

Instructions regarding War Diaries and Intelligence Summaries are contained in F. S. Regs., Part II. and the Staff Manual respectively. Title pages will be prepared in manuscript.

Place	Date	Hour	Summary of Events and Information	Remarks and references to Appendices
RONNY	1.8.16	6 a.m.	Moved off in rear of 8th Cav Field Amb to starting point W of LAMEVILLE. Thence via DAOURS, AMEINS, north of River SOMME to PICQUIGNY and bivouacing for the night at ST PIERRE a GOUY. Evacuated 10 horses to No 12 Mob. Vety Sectn.	
St PIERRE à GOUY	2.8.16 9 a.m		Moved off in rear of 8th Cav. Fd Amb. to starting point Railway bridge at HANGEST. Thence via BOURDON, FLIXECOURT, AILLY, ST RIQUIER, AILLENCOURT to NEVILLY L'HOPITAL — Bivouaced in field — with supply ld.	
NEVILLY L'HOPITAL	3.8.16		Cleaning up & catering round saddlery — Received orders that we should move next day. Evacuated 10 horses by road to ABBEVILLE	
"	4.8.16 6:20 a.m		Moved off to starting point bivo. sheets end of CANCHY in rear of 8th Cav to last. Thence via MARCHEVILLE, CRECY, LIEGESCOURT to DOURIEZ. Bivouaced in field on the bank of the river.	
DOURIEZ	5.8.16 10.30 a.m		Moved off in rear of 8th Cav. Fd. Amb. to starting point bivo. Pont Point 84. Thence via GUIGNY, S.E. of HESDIN to BLINGEL — Bivouaced in field.	
BLINGEL	6.8.16 7.8.16		Routine Routine	

Instructions regarding War Diaries and Intelligence Summaries are contained in F. S. Regs., Part II. and the Staff Manual respectively. Title pages will be prepared in manuscript.

WAR DIARY
or
INTELLIGENCE SUMMARY.
(Erase heading not required.)

20 Mobile Vety Section.

Army Form C. 2118.

Place	Date	Hour	Summary of Events and Information	Remarks and references to Appendices
BLINGEL	8.8.16		Routine.	
″	9.8.16		Evacuated 17 horses to NEUFCHATEL	
″	10.8.16		Routine	
″	11.8.16		Routine SE2980 Pte Cross admitted to Hospital.	
″	12.8.16		Routine	
″	13.8.16		Routine	
″	14.8.16		13 horses evacuated to NEUFCHATEL	
″	15.8.16		Inspection of Transport by O.C. A.S.C 3rd Cav. Div.	
″	16.8.16		Routine.	
″	17.8.16		Routine	
″	18.8.16		Routine	
″	19.8.16		Routine	
″	20.8.16		Routine.	
″	21.8.16		Evacuated 15 horses to NEUFCHATEL	
″	23.8.16		Routine.	
″	24.8.16		Routine.	

T2134. Wt. W708—776. 500000. 4/15. Sir J. C. & S.

WAR DIARY
or
INTELLIGENCE SUMMARY.
(Erase heading not required.)

Army Form C. 2118.

2 O Mtr Victy Coy

Place	Date	Hour	Summary of Events and Information	Remarks and references to Appendices
BLANGEL	25.8.16		Routine. SE 2950 Pte Owen returned from Hospital.	
	26.8.16		Routine.	
	27.8.16		Routine. 19 O/Rs WMCs evacuated to NEUF CHATEL.	
	28.8.16		SE 16466 Pte Jenkins reported his arrival for duty from St Omer (Mil. Hospital).	
	29.8.16		Routine.	
	30.8.16		Routine.	
	31.8.16		Routine. 14 Cars WMCs evacuated to ABBEVILLE.	

3e

Instructions regarding War Diaries and Intelligence Summaries are contained in F.S. Regs., Part II. and the Staff Manual respectively. Title pages will be prepared in manuscript.

WAR DIARY
or
INTELLIGENCE SUMMARY.

20 Mobile Vety Section.

Army Form C. 2118.

Vol 19

(Erase heading not required.)

Place	Date	Hour	Summary of Events and Information	Remarks and references to Appendices
BLINGEL	1.9.16	—	Routine work.	
"	2.9.16	—	Routine work.	
"	3.9.16	—	Routine	
"	4.9.16	—	13 sick horses evacuated HESDIN - NEUFCHATEL	
"	5.9.16	—	Routine	
"	6.9.16	—	17 cast horses evacuated to the Remount Rod Section FREVENT.	
"	7.9.16	—	Routine	
"	8.9.16	—	Routine	
"	9.9.16	—	26 sick horses evacuated HESDIN - NEUFCHATEL. Received orders that this Appendix A. Brigade would move next day to the DOURIEZ area. This section would march independently. Received orders from A.D.V.S. to collect ten horses from VERCHIN Sent linkers with led horses for in advance to the new area under Lieut. TEBB.	
"	10.9.16	10 a.m.	Moved off with the rest of the section in rear of the brigade via MARCONNE, GUIGNY to DOURIEZ — occupied the same bivouac as on the journey up to BLINGEL — Weather fine — Water supply good, close to a stream.	
DOURIEZ 2.		9 a.m.	Received orders for next days march.	

Army Form C. 2118.

WAR DIARY
or
INTELLIGENCE SUMMARY. 26 Mobile Vety Section

(Erase heading not required.)

Instructions regarding War Diaries and Intelligence Summaries are contained in F.S. Regs., Part II. and the Staff Manual respectively. Title pages will be prepared in manuscript.

Place	Date	Hour	Summary of Events and Information	Remarks and references to Appendices
DOURIEZ	11.9.16	10 a.m.	Numbers & sick horses moved off to new area.	
		12 noon	Moved off also but soon caught up the 8th Cav. Field Amb- Bivouac via CRECY, DOMVAST, to ST. RIQUIER.	APP. B.
		5 p.m.	Arrived ST. RIQUIER.- Sent round a message to send all horses for evacuation into the Section during the night. Bivouaced in an orchard - Weather fine - Received return for tomorrows	
ST. RIQUIER	12.9.16	8.30 a.m.	Sent a corporal with four men to N0.22 Vety. Hospital ABBEVILLE with 10 sick horses with orders to join up in the evening.	
		6.30 a.m.	Moved off with Section in rear of the 6th Cav. Fd. Amb. via AILLY - FLIXECOURT LA CHAUSSEE to ST. SAUVEUR - Raining most of the way - Bivouaced in a field - Very dirty bivouac.	APP. C.
ST. SAUVEUR		4 p.m.	Arrived in bivouac	
ST. SAUVEUR	13.9.16		Stayed in bivouac all day & cleaned up - Received orders for tomorrows march.	
ST. SAUVEUR	14.9.16	6.45	Moved off in rear of 8th Cav. Fd. Amb. to starting point Proceeded via AMIENS RIVERIE CAMON to a point S.W. of QUERRIEU, where the Whole Brigade assembled & fed - Proceeded later in the day to bivouac	APP. D.

WAR DIARY
or
INTELLIGENCE SUMMARY.   20 Mobile Vety Sec.

(Erase heading not required.)

Army Form C. 2118.

Place	Date	Hour	Summary of Events and Information	Remarks and references to Appendices
BUSSY LES DAOURS.	14.9.16	3 p.m.	Arrived in bivouac lately occupied by Indian Cav. Div. Received orders about this next way to utilise the Mobile Vety Section of a Cavalry Division. Informed that this Section would be in its rear Section. Collected horses from this bivouac. Proceeded to make arrangements for the Evacuation of Horses from CORBIE next day.	
"	15.9.16		Mobile Vety Section (now divisionalised under A.D.V.S. – during received no definite orders) proceeded with Section 7 Div to horses via BUSSY - DAOURS. - LA NEUVILLE to CORBIE - Red A.T.V.S. 3rd Cav. Div. with A.D.V.S. Bw. Corps. at LA NEUVILLE & received orders to bivouac section there. Evacuated 24 sick horses CORBIE to FORGES - LES - EAUX. & returned to bivouac with the rest of the Brigade at LA NEUVILLE. Joined later in the day by 13 & 14 Mob. Vety Sections.	APP. "E"
LA NEUVILLE	16.9.16		Standing to all day expecting to move at any minute. Collected horses from the bivouac. Received orders that the Brigade would move back tomorrow.	
"	17.9.16		Evacuated 33 sick horses CORBIE to FORGES, LES, EAUX - returned with Section to a stable field S of VECQUEMONT. where we bivouaced with the 6th Cav. Fd. Amb.	APP. "E"

2353 Wt. W2544/1454 700,000 5/15 D. D. & L.   A.D.S.S./Form/C. 2118.

WAR DIARY or INTELLIGENCE SUMMARY

Army Form C. 2118.

20 Mob. Vety. Section

Place	Date	Hour	Summary of Events and Information	Remarks and references to Appendices
VECQUEMONT	17.9.16	—	Sgt NORRIS with 9 men reported his arrival for duty from No 19 Vety Hospital – This NCO & these men were to provide consulting future –	OR
"	18.9.16		Burie a general routine – Raining heavily	
"	19.9.16		Routine – Raining heavily – Moved thirds ab FRECHENCOURT.	
"	20.9.16		Evacuated 27 sick horses FRECHENCOURT – FORGES-LES-EAUX. The men from 19 Vety Hospital were useless to lead horses to the station unless they walked themselves – to railhead were some distance away this was no advisable – took him to railhead in a limber. These men had had no experience of horses. Whatever could not have rendered much assistance to a road in difficulties in a truck. Raining heavily all day – All the horses of the Brigade were standing in mud over the fetlocks – Very cold at night. Pte KING A.H. – Pte CLEGG J.H. reported sick there admitted to hospital and evacuated to the Base.	OR OR OR OR
VECQUEMONT	21.9.16		Received orders that we should probably move WEST next day. Received orders from A.D.V.S. Cav. Corps to station the attached Sergeans & nine men to the SECUNDERABAD Mob. Vety. So.	OR

WAR DIARY
or
INTELLIGENCE SUMMARY. 20 Mt. Vety. Sec.

Army Form C. 2118.

Place	Date	Hour	Summary of Events and Information	Remarks and references to Appendices
NECQUEMONT	22.9.16		Evacuated 7 sick horses. BIRBIE - FORGES LES EAUX.	
		9 a.m.	Moved off in rear of 8th Cav. Fd. Amb. via LA MOTTE. CAMON. AMIENS. AILLY	APP. "G"
			PICQUIGNY to bivouac at L'ETOILE.	
L'ETOILE		5 h.m.	Arrived in bivouac in a swamp.	
L'ETOILE	23.9.16	4 h.m.	Received orders for next days move.	
		8.30 a.m.	Moved off in rear of 8 Cav. F.A. via BRUCAMPS - DOMQUEUR - CRAMONT - CONTEVILLE.	APP "H"
			AUXI LE CHATEAU - RUIR to ROUGEFAY.	
ROUGEFAY		4 h.m.	Arrived at ROUGEFAY & bivouaced in a field - Received horses for evacuation other than	
			we took with us next day - Lt Elliott reported sick runs not able to ride	
			next day.	
ROUGEFAY	24.9.16	5 a.m.	Moved off in rear of 8 Cav. Fd. Amb. via HESDIN. PLUMOISON. MARESQUEL - CAMPAGNE	
			LES HESDIN to BOIS JEAN - Bivouaced in a field 6 kilometres from this nearest	APP. "J"
			regimental town 20 kilometres from railhead - Water supply poor - only ponds.	
		5 h.m.	Reached bivouac.	
BOIS JEAN	25.9.16		Lt Elliott admitted to Hospital - Cleaning up.	
			Horses admitted for evacuation - Found that horses would be accepted at	
	26.9.16		MONTREUIL for evacuation - Only 6 kilometres away.	

Army Form C. 2118.

WAR DIARY
or
INTELLIGENCE SUMMARY. 20 Mit. Vety Sec.
(Erase heading not required.)

Instructions regarding War Diaries and Intelligence Summaries are contained in F. S. Regs., Part II. and the Staff Manual respectively. Title pages will be prepared in manuscript.

Place	Date	Hour	Summary of Events and Information	Remarks and references to Appendices
BOIS JEAN	27.9.16		Evacuated 14 sick horses AINTREVIL to NEUFCHATEL.	DR
"	28.9.16		Routine.	DR
"	29.9.16		Routine – Evacuated 14 sick horses MONTREUIL to NEUFCHATEL.	DR
"	30.9.16		Moved to billets at BEAURAIN CHATEAU. Very good billets in the hills & the hymne river – Close to the river. Unfortunately the village contained often mills and as its wood used in its construction who highly inflamed we were over throne.	DR

Appendix A.

B.M. 88/4.

Officer Commanding,
 Royal Horse Guards.   G. Battery, R.H.A.
 Tenth Royal Hussars.   8th Cav Fld Ambce.
 Essex Yeomanry.   20th Mob Vetery Sectn.
 8th Machine Gun Sqd.   Capt Harford.
 2/Lt Hann.   Supply Officer.
 — 8th Signal Troop.

---

1. Brigade will march as under tomorrow 10th inst.
 (a) Brigade Starting Point T roads just S. of 2nd G. of GRIGNY.
  Time 2 p.m.
 (b) Order of march 10th Hussars, 8th M.G.Sqdn, 8th C.F.A. Essex Yeo, R.H.Gds and G Battery.

2. Assemble 10th Hussars head at Starting Point tail towards AUCHY, Remaining units in rear of 10th Hussars, order as above.

3. Routes – 10th Hussars, 8th M.G.Sqdn, 8th C.F.A. via HESDIN– MOURIEZ– TORTEFONTAINE road. Remainder of Brigade via MARCONNE– GUIGNY– DOMPIERRE road, diverging from the rest at X roads S. of B D of HESDIN, from here onwards units will march independently to their billets.
 NOTE. (a) G Battery will fall in behind R.H.G's as they pass GRIGNY
    (b) M.G.Sqdn cross river AUTHIE at MOULMEL.

4. "A" Echelons will accompany units and will NOT be brigaded.
    move off from   12. noon.
5. *"B" Echelon/rendezvous head at AUCHY station/11-60 a.m. marching thence under Capt Harford, order of march as above, picking up G Battery echelon en route.

6. 20th Mobile Veterinary Sectn will march independently.

7. Billetting area:-
 Bde H.Q.   LIGESCOURT.   R.H.G's & G Battery, PONCHES-
                      ESTRUVAL.
 8th M.G.Sqdn ESTRUVAL.   10th Hussars, 8th C.F.A. &
                 20th M.Vety Sect.   DOURIEZ.
 Essex Yeo, MOULMEL & RAPCHY.

 Dismounted Parties will proceed to AUCHY under regimental arrangements. Here they will come under Command of Capt Gordon Canning, 10th Hussars, Mule transport will evacuate the Tents and Dismounted men of the R.H.G's to AUCHY. Capt Gordon Canning will arrange for a place for the storage of the Tents near the Station so that they can be loaded on the train on the 14th to accompany the Dismounted Party, he will also arrange for the parties to be billetted in AUCHY.

               S.J.HARDY, Captain,
9/9/16.   Brigade Major, 8th Cavalry Brigade.

* Units can send their "B" echelon on before 12 noon if they wish, to water and feed at AUCHY.

Notes. 1. British warms will be carried rolled behind the saddle. Waterproof sheets (with lace or string) fo fitted to be carried over wallets, 2nd blanket under saddle, change of washing carried wherever unit commanders prefer.
 2. A Echelon on scale A, but only 2 picks and 2 shovels on each regimental limber, remainder on B echelon.
 Brigade reserve tool wagon remains & with R.H.Gds.
 3. March will be continued 11th, 12th and 13th.
 4. No troops may pass HESDIN before 1 p.m.

```
Officer Commanding,                                      B.M. 92.
   Royal Horse Gds.        G Battery.
   10th Hussars.           8th Cav Fld Ambce.
   Essex Yeo.              20th Mob Vety Sect.      AM. B.
   8th Machine Gun Sqd.    Capt Harford.
                           Supply Officer.
```

1 Brigade will move tomorrow 11th inst, in two columns as under:-
(A) No 1. Column order of march R.H.Gds, 10th Hussars, 8th M.G.Sqd &
    8th C.F.A., Starting Point --- Church at LIGESCOURT, 1. p.m.

   Route.   CRECY--- DOMVAST--- MILLENCOURT.

   Note. Units must use most direct road to Ligescourt from their
          billets. M.G.Sqd must allow 10th Hussars to pass and then
          cut in behind them and in front of 8th C.F.A. on the way to
          Starting Point.

(B) No 2 Column order of march Essex Yeo, G Battery.
       Starting Point X roads ½ mile S. of DOMPIERRE time 1. p.m.
   Route. WADICOURT--- E of ESTREES --- NOYELLE en CHAUSSEE --- GAPENNES
           St. RIQUIER.
       This column will be under Colonel WHITMORE, Essex Yeo.

2. A echelon accompany units.

3. (a) B echelon Starting Point X roads at N. exit of CRECY. Time
        11 . a.m.   March under Capt HANFORD, R.H.G's by same
        route as column No 1.

    (b) Billeting parties must leave guides to meet their B echelons
        at X roads North of M. of MILLENCOURT by 1-15 p.m.

4.   Billeting parties meet Staff Captain at X roads just N. of M
        MILLENCOURT at 12 noon.

                                   S.J.HARDY,   Captain,
10/9/16.   Brigade Major, 8th Cavalry Brigade.

Notes. 1. The 1st Indian Cavalry Division will not be clear of new
           area before 2 p.m.
        2. March will be continued on 12th, 13th & 14th Septr.
        3. Other 2 Brigades of Division are behind us. Echelons must
           therefore keep closed up to their units.
        4. 20th Mobile Veterinary Sectn will proceed independently

B.M. 94.

A.P.P.C.

Officer Commanding,
Royal Horse Gds.   G.Battery.
10th Hussars.   8th C.F.A.
Essex Yeo.   20th M.V.S.
8th M.G.Sqd.   Capt Harford.
2/Lt Mann.   Staff Captain.
        Supply Officer.

1. The Brigade will march tomorrow 12th inst as follows to an area St SAUVEUR ARGOEUVES remaining there the night 12/13th and 13/14th, thence on 14th to Y area S.W. of VECQUEMONT.
   (a) Brigade Starting Point X roads at W. end of YAUCOURT, Time 8-45 a.m.
   (b) Order of march 10th Hussars, R.H.G's Essex, M.G.Sqd, G Battery, 8th C.F.A. "A" echelon, 20th M.V.S. "B" echelon.
   (c) Route. AILLY --- FLIXECOURT --- LA CHAUSSEE.
   (d) Assemble as follows 10th Hussars head at Starting Point, tail towards BUIGNY. R.H.Gds head at Starting Point tail towards St Riquier, remaining units in order of march behind R.H.Gds.

2. "A" echelon will accompany units to Starting Point, there be collected as usual and Brigaded under 2/Lt Mann.

3. "B" echelon. 10th Hussars B echelon will not follow the regiment, but will use the Southern NEUF MOULIN road, closing up as soon as it can on to the R.H.Gds B echelon, Capt Harford will take charge at NEUF MOULIN, as soon as it is closed up on the R.H.Gds B echelon, Capt Harford will take charge, picking up Machine Gun Sqdn echelon as he passes DRUGY, & that of the other units of the Brigade at X roads N. of second U of St MAUGHILLE. Essex & G Battery & C.F.A. will have their B echelons drawn up just N. of that point as soon as possible after their main bodies are clear.

                                S.J.HARDY, Captain,
11/9/16.   Brigade Major, 9th Cavalry Brigade.

Notes. (a) 10th Hussars must come to Starting Point via VAUCHELLES, R.H.Gds through the Wood DRUGY and South of the Station, 8th Machine Gun Sqdn by same route when R.H.Gds are clear.

       (b) M.G.Sqd must arrange independently with Essex and G Battery so that he falls into column behind the Essex.

       (c) The Brigade will water at FLIXECOURT. Each regiment will send an officer (and an Interpreter if possible) to arrange with the Mayor and inhabitants to have water laid out in tubs and buckets the whole depth of the Town route through the Town, which heads of Brigade should reach at 10-30 a.m.

       (d) Billetting Parties meet the Staff Captain at Church at St SAUVEUR at 11 a.m.

       (e) The 7th Brigade marches in rear of us Starting from St RIQUIER 9 a.m. Its fighting troops may pass our B echelon on the road if they wish to.

Officer Commanding,
Royal Horse Gds.   8th Cav Fld Amb.
Tenth Hussars.   20th M.V.Sect.
Essex Yeo.   Capt. Harford.
8th M.G.Sqd.   2/Lt Hann.
G.Battery.   Staff Captain.
Supply Officer.   A.D.C.

1. Brigade moves tomorrow 14th to "X" area, now occupied by 2nd Indian Cavalry Division, North of BUSSY as follows:-
(a) Brigade Starting Point - a Point on the main road about 1000 yards E. of Eastern exit of ARGOEUVES, just S. of the U of ARGOEUVES.   Time 7 a.m.

(b) Order of March- R.H.Gds, Essex, 10th Hussars, 8th M.G.Sqd. G.Battery, 8th C.F.A. "A" echelon 20th M.V.S.

(c) Route. N. outskirts of AMIENS -- RIVERY -- CAMON.

2. Brigade will water just W. of LAMOTTE, and after watering will move via LAMOTTE, past T roads one mile N. of LAMOTTE to a suitable off saddling place W. of their eventual bivouacs which will be in valley about ½ mile S. of QUERRIEU.

3. "A" echelon will be handed over as usual and Brigaded under 2/Lt HANN as units pass Starting Point.

4. (a) "B" echelon march Divisionalised under Senior Brigade Transport Officer. 8th Bde Transport joins the column at ARGOEUVES behind Divisional Troops "B" echelon, xxxxxxxxx so that order of B Echelons will be Divisional Troops, 8th, 6th, 7th, Brigades.
   After watering W of LAMOTTE, they follow Divisional Ammunition Column to Q of VECQUEMONT and rejoin Brigades in X area bivouac as soon as a Divisional Staff Officer reports road to BUSSY clear.
(b) "B" Echelon of Essex Yeomanry, Machine Gun Squadron, R.H.A. and C.F.A. will move off from ST. SAUVEUR as soon as fighting troops are clear of ST. SAUVEUR, and park on the 10th. Hussars camping ground.
   "B" Echelons of other units at ARGOEUVES will also assemble here.
(c) Divisional Troops "B" Echelon may be expected to pass here about 10.45 a.m.

5.   Billets will to be taken over direct from the Indian Cavalry under orders to be issued by the Staff Captain.

                                    S.J.HARDY Captain, Bde. Major,
13/9/16.   8th. Cavalry Brigade.

NOTES.(1) Before watering all units will close up in mass formation close to watering place so as not to block units in rear.
     (11) All units to be E of CAMON by 2 p.m.
     (111) 6th. and 7th. Brigades are behind us and water after us.

APP. "E"
B.M. 100/1.

Officer Commanding,
Royal Horse Gds.   ~~8th Cav Fld Ambce.~~
10th Hussars.   20th M.V.Sect.
Essex Yeo.   2/Lt Hann.
8th M.G.Sqd.   Capt Harford.
"G" Batty, R.H.A.   Staff Captain.
Supply Officer.   A.D.C.
            8th Signal Troop.

1. The Brigade will move tomorrow under "B" scale as lately amended by S.C. 2032 of 13/9/16.

2. (a) <u>Starting Point</u>   T roads 200 yards North of T in VECQUEMONT, Time 8-45 a.m.

   (b) <u>Order of March</u>   Essex, R.H.Gds, 10th Hussars, 8th M.G.Sqd, "G" Batty and Mobile Section of 8th C.F.A..

   (c) <u>Route</u>   O of DAOURS to LA NEUVILLE.

   (d) <u>Assembly Area</u>   W. and N.W. of LA NEUVILLE.

3. (a) The Division will move via DAOURS and eventually form 2 columns at BONNAY and LA NEUVILLE respectively at 11 a.m.
       The BONNAY column ---- 7th and 6th Brigades.
       The LA NEUVILLE column, 8th Bde and Div'nl Troops.

4. (a) Mobile Vety Sectns will be collected and march under orders of A.D.V.S.
   (b) Mobile Section of C.F.A. accompany Brigade.
       Heavy Sections of C.F.A. divisionalised under orders of A.D.M.S.
       (This includes G.S.Wagons of C.F.A. and Motor Ambulances).

5. (a) "A" echelon will accompany units.
       "B" echelons remain in present area and come under orders of O.C. A.S.C. for movements.

                                   S.J.HARDY. Captain,
                              Brigade Major, 8th Cavalry Brigade

NOTES. (1) 6th and 7th Brigades are in front of us, -- order of march 7th, 6th Brigades and have same Starting Point.

       (ii) Water bottles must be filled before leaving the BONNAY-- LA NEUVILLE area.

       (iii) HOTCHKISS ammunition in clips will be carried as arranged when Brigade was at BONNAY last.

14/9/16.

6.6.

APP. F. 20th M.V.S.

BM109/1
17/9/16

1. The Brigade will move to new bivouac S of VECQUEMONT today 17th inst.
(a) Starting Point — LL of LA NEUVILLE, Time 7 A.M.
(b) Order of March — R H Gds, 10th Hussars, Essex Yeo, 8th M.G. Sqd, "G" Batty, mobile section of 8th C.F.A, and 20th M.V. Sect.
(c) Route — Via O of DAOURS.

2. "A" echelon to accompany units.

3. Tents will be packed & handed over to the Quartermaster of 10th Hussars, alongside the DAOURS — LA NEUVILLE road, about 100 yards West of the Cross roads at Starting point, he will leave a guard with them of 1 N.C.O. & 2 men till 8.30 a.m, when lorries will fetch them.

17/9/16.
1-15 a.m.

Sd. S.G. Hardy, Capt.
Bde Major 8 Cav Bde

Note (i) The C.F.A and 20th M.V.S. will join Column as it passes their bivouac.
(ii) "B" echelon will march via BUSSY to VECQUEMONT to rejoin units in fresh bivouac by 8.45 a.m.

Officer Commanding,
  Royal Horse Guards.   8th Cav Fld Ambce.
  Tenth Royal Hussars. 20th Mob Vety.Sect.
  Essex Yeomanry.   2/Lt Hann.
  8th Machine Gun Sqd. Staff Captain.
  G.Battery, R.H.A.   A.D.C.
  Supply Officer.   Brigade Transport Officer.

B.M. 118/1.

APP. "G"

1. Brigade moves tomorrow as under.

   STARTING POINT. T. roads just N.of VECQUEMONT. Time 9 a.m.

   ORDER of MARCH. 10th Hussars, Essex, R.H.Gds, 8th M.G.Sqd, G Batty, "A" echelon, 8th C.F.A., 20th M.V.S.

   ROUTE. LA MOTTE -- CAMON-- AMIENS Station -- AILLY -- PICQUIGNY, keeping South of the River SOMME as far as possible.

2. (a) "A" echelon will be collected by 2/Lt HANN, just South of Railway bridge at exit of Camp and march brigaded.

   (b) "B" echelon will be collected by Lt SMITH and handed over to the 7th Brigade Transport Officer at the Starting Point at 2-20 p.m., and will march Divisionalised and billet as a unit on night 22/23rd at St PIERRE A GOUY.

3. Billeting area. BOUCHON --L'ETOILE.
   Representatives meet the Staff Captain at Church atv L'ETOILE at 12 noon.

4. Units will each send a representative (the 10th Hussars to send a Captain) to arrange water near AILLY SUR SOMME, where they should meet the Officer detailed by 10th Hussars at 10-45 a.m.

21/9/16.
                                    S.J.HARDY, Captain,
                         Brigade Major, 8th Cavalry Brigade.

NOTE.
    Motor ambulances move under orders of A.D.M.S., *Brigade well* march 5 miles per hour.

    7th and 6th Brigades are on same road in rear of us.

20 NWL   All Units and   APP. H.
                 2/2ⁿ Hann.   BM 119/1

1. Brigade will march 23ʳᵈ as under
   a. <u>Starting Point</u> the most Northerly T roads in VAUCHELLES
                    les-DOMART.   Time 9. a.m.
   b. <u>Order of March</u>. Essex. R. Hgds. X.R.H. 8ᵗʰ M.G.Sqd, G. Batty,
                 8ᵗʰ C.F.A. "A" echelon, 20ᵗʰ M.V.S.
   c. <u>Route</u>.   BRUCAMPS-DOMQUEUR-CRAMONT-
                   CONTEVILLE - AUXI LE CHATEAU - BUIRE.
   d. <u>Billeting Area</u> FILLIÈVRES - AUBROMETZ - MONCHEL -
                   CONCHY-SUR-CANCHE - ROUGEFAY.

2. a. "A" echelon will be handed over at Starting Point
      and march Brigaded under 2/2ⁿ Hann.
   b. "B" echelons billet at FROHEN LE PETIT.

3. Divisional Headquarters move to FROHEN LE GRAND.

4. Essex Yeo. will send a Captain and other units a
   subaltern to make watering arrangements at
   AUXI LE CHATEAU, to rendezvous at S.W. exit
   of Auxi le Chateau at 10.30 a.m.

5. Billeting Parties meet the Staff Captain at Church at
   ROUGEFAY at eleven a.m.

                               S.J.Hardy   Captain.
22-9-16   Brigade Major 8ᵗʰ Cav Bde.

<u>NOTE</u> (1) Essex and X.R.H. at BOUCHON must come to
        Starting Point by road via MOUFLERS and just
        S.E. of the word "Chau".
        Other units at L'ÉTOILE will march via LA
        FOLIE and the S.E. entrance to VAUCHELLES.

    (11) Head of Brigade not to cross DOULLENS-AUXI-LE-
        CHATEAU road before 12 noon.

6.6

R.H.G.	8th CFA
X R H	20th M.V.S.
E Y	2/7th Hussars
8th M.G. Sqd	A.D.C.
G Batty	Staff Capt.

B.M. / 19/4

APP. "J"

1. Bde moves 24th as under
   STARTING PT   CHURCH at GALAMETZ   8.30 AM
   Order of March   RHGs X RH EY 8th MG Sqn
        G Batty A Echelon 8 CFA 20 MVS

2. Billeting Area South of R. CANCHE only
   PLUMOISON   BOUIN   AUBIN ST VAAST
   ECQUEMICOURT   MARESQUEL   BEAURAINVILLE
   L'ESPINOY   BOIS JEAN - Chateau REMONT
   LA NEUVILLE   LAMBUS

3. A Echelon will be collected as usual on passing S.P.

6. B Echelon rejoins unit night 24/25th

4. Billeting parties meet S.C. at Church
   PLUMOISON   11 AM.

S.P. Hardy Capt
Bde Maj 8 CB
23.9.16

Note: Campagne ho Hesdin and Hotel Moderne at Beaurainville must not be used as billets.

Army Form C. 2118.

WAR DIARY
or
INTELLIGENCE SUMMARY.
(Erase heading not required.)

20 Mob. Vety Section.

Vol 20

Place	Date	Hour	Summary of Events and Information	Remarks and references to Appendices
BEAURAIN CHATEAU	1.10.16	—	Routine – Received orders to move to BRIMEUX following day. Section packed up ready to move by 12 noon to await billets – SE. 8054 Pte NUTTERY.	PR
"	2.10.16	—	SE. 4395 Pte WOLSTENHOLME R. reported for duty from No 3 Vety Hospital.	PR
"		12 noon	Section moved off along main road to BRIMEUX. Downpour of rain – horses picketed in a field but found shelter for the artillery & a room for the men.	PR
BRIMEUX	3.10.16	—	Routine – Looking round to see the horses under cover & weather very bad.	PR
"	4.10.16	—	Managed to get all the horses under cover.	PR
"	5.10.16	—	Routine	PR
"	6.10.16	—	Routine	PR
"	7.10.16	—	Routine	PR
"	8.10.16	—	Routine – Evacuated 18 sick horses from MONTREUIL to NEUCHATEL	PR
"	9.10.16	—	Routine – Received orders to attach 3 horse flans from No 5 Vety Hospital ABBEVILLE	PR
"	10.10.16	—	Routine	PR
"	11.10.16	—	Routine – Evacuated 10 sick horses to No 22 Vety Hospital ABBEVILLE – Cpl Kiftomes & one man forming conducting party & with orders to return with flans to this Section.	PR

WAR DIARY
or
INTELLIGENCE SUMMARY. 20 Mobile Vety Section.

(Erase heading not required.)

Army Form C. 2118.

Place	Date	Hour	Summary of Events and Information	Remarks and references to Appendices
BRIMEUX	12.10.16		Routine.	
"	13.10.16		Routine.	
"	14.10.16		Routine.	
"	15.10.16		Routine.	
"	16.10.16		Routine.	
"	17.10.16		Routine. H/horses evacuated to NEUFCHATEL from MONTREUIL	
"	18.10.16		Routine. SE 3864 Pte NEWMAN R.J. appointed shoeing smith from 4.10.16 Local Corps Order 570	
"	19.10.16		Routine	
"	20.10.16		Routine. - SE 4697 L.Smth SIGLEY orders to join 44 Mobile Vety Section. T 5/689/16 A.V.C. Records	
"	21.10.16		Routine. H/horses evacuated MONTREUIL to NEUFCHATEL	
"	22.10.16		Routine.	
"	23.10.16		Routine.- Received orders to move Section to HESMOND.	
"	24.10.16		Section packed up ready to move to HESMOND, but on arrival of the billeting party it was found that the billets were occupied by other troops - ordered to remain where we were. Ready packed up - Received orders that the R.V.S. Can. Corps would visit Section 10.30.25.10.16 standing to alertting. He Refused to move. Received orders from the following day to HESMOND.	
"	25.10.16	2.30	Received notice that the D.D.V.S. Can Corps agreed visit the section must of woods unable to be moved. Ordered to go billeting to HESMOND.	

WAR DIARY
or
INTELLIGENCE SUMMARY. 20 Mobile Vety Sectn.

Army Form C. 2118.

(Erase heading not required.)

Instructions regarding War Diaries and Intelligence Summaries are contained in F. S. Regs. Part II. and the Staff Manual respectively. Title pages will be prepared in manuscript.

Place	Date	Hour	Summary of Events and Information	Remarks and references to Appendices
BRIMEUX.	26.10.16	10.a.m	Section moved to new billets at HESMOND. nr BEAURAINVILLE. LOISON OFFR.	
HESMOND	27.10.16	-	Very good billets with fm horse gmn.	
"	28.10.16	-	Routine - Improving stables & billets	
"	29.10.16	-	Routine.	
"			Routine - Escorted 6 horses HESDIN - NEUFCHATEL - SE 439S- Pte R. WOLSTENHOLME	
			turned over to M.M.P. from Rlu to undergo 42 days field Punishment No 1. awarded	
			by sentence of a Courts martial.	
"	30.10.16		Routine.	
"	31.10.16		Routine.	

Army Form C. 2118.

WAR DIARY
or
INTELLIGENCE SUMMARY. 20 Mobile V.By.&c.

(Erase heading not required.)

Instructions regarding War Diaries and Intelligence Summaries are contained in F. S. Regs., Part II. and the Staff Manual respectively. Title pages will be prepared in manuscript.

Vol 2

Place	Date	Hour	Summary of Events and Information	Remarks and references to Appendices
HESMOND	1.11.16		Routine.	
	2.11.16		Routine.	
	3.11.16		Routine.	
	4.11.16		4 horses evacuated BEAUVRANVILLE to NEUFCHATEL	
	5.11.16		Routine - training cleaning up billets & stables & improving them	
	6.11.16		Routine.	
	7.11.16		Routine.	
	8.11.16		Routine.	
	9.11.16		Routine.	
	10.11.16		Routine.	
	11.11.16		Routine.	
	12.11.16		Routine.	
	13.11.16		Routine.	
	14.11.16		Routine.	
	15.11.16		Routine. SE 8462 Pte NAWTIN reported his arrival from N°3 V.By posted to Replace SE A395 Pte WOLSTENHOLME	

Army Form C. 2118.

WAR DIARY
or
INTELLIGENCE SUMMARY. 20 Mob. Vety Sec.
(Erase heading not required.)

Instructions regarding War Diaries and Intelligence Summaries are contained in F. S. Regs., Part II. and the Staff Manual respectively. Title pages will be prepared in manuscript.

Place	Date	Hour	Summary of Events and Information	Remarks and references to Appendices
AESMOND	16.11.16		Routine.	
"	17.11.16		Routine.	
"	18.11.16		Routine.	
"	19.11.16		Sick horses evacuated MARESQUEL to NEUFCHATEL	
"	20.11.16		Routine.	
"	21.11.16		Routine.	
"	22.11.16		Routine. SE 21962 Pte ROLFE W.G. joined from 23 Vety Hospital to replace	
"			SE 6286 Pte Ryan M.	
"	23.11.16		Routine.	
"	24.11.16		Routine.	
"	25.11.16		Routine. SE 6286 Pte RYAN. M. invalided to join 23 Vety Hospital	
"	26.11.16		Routine.	
"	27.11.16		Routine.	
"	28.11.16		Routine.	
"	29.11.16		Routine.	
"	30.11.16		Routine.	

Army Form C. 2118.

WAR DIARY
or
INTELLIGENCE SUMMARY.
(Erase heading not required.)

Instructions regarding War Diaries and Intelligence Summaries are contained in F. S. Regs., Part II. and the Staff Manual respectively. Title pages will be prepared in manuscript.

N° Mobile Vety Section.   Vol 22

Place	Date	Hour	Summary of Events and Information	Remarks and references to Appendices
HESMOND	1.12.16	Routine		
"	2.12.16	Routine	24 horses evacuated MARESQUEL to NEUFCHATEL	
"	3.12.16	Routine		
"	4.12.16	Routine		
"	5.12.16	Routine		
"	6.12.16	Routine		
"	7.12.16	Routine		
"	8.12.16	Routine	Pte WOLSTENHOLME SE 4395, Arrived Eg'pm N°3 Vety Hospital.	
"	9.12.16	Routine	8 horses evacuated MARESQUEL to NEUFCHATEL	
"	10.12.16	Routine		
"	11.12.16	Routine		
"	12.12.16	Routine		
"	13.12.16	Routine		
"	14.12.16	Routine		
"	15.12.16	Routine		
"	16.12.16	Routine	5 horses evacuated MARESQUEL to NEUFCHATEL	

Army Form C. 2118.

WAR DIARY
or
INTELLIGENCE SUMMARY. 20 Mobile Vety Section
(Erase heading not required.)

Instructions regarding War Diaries and Intelligence Summaries are contained in F. S. Regs., Part II. and the Staff Manual respectively. Title pages will be prepared in manuscript.

Place	Date	Hour	Summary of Events and Information	Remarks and references to Appendices
AESMONDT	26		Routine	
"	16.12.16		Routine	
"		9.p.m	Routine	
"		30.p.m	Routine - Received orders that Section would move to 22.12.16	
"		31.2.m	Routine - Evacuated & drew MARESQUEL to NEUFCHATEL - Received orders for Mp.A.	
"			any following day.	
"	22 Dec 1916		Section moved in full marching order with wagons Public Evacuated via BEAURAINVILLE	Mp.A.
"			BRIMEUX BEAUMERIE ECUIRES SORRUS ST JOSSE CAPELLE & billets at	
"			CUCQ taking over billets occupied by 13 Mob Vety Sec. Averency - Beauguen	
"			all the way.	
CUCQ		1 a.m	arrived in billets.	
CUCQ	22.12.16		Brightening up billets	
"	24.12.16		Routine.	
"	25.12.16		Xmas is a Sunday.	
"	26.12.16		Routine.	
"	27.12.16		Routine.	

WAR DIARY
or
INTELLIGENCE SUMMARY.
(Erase heading not required.)

Army Form C. 2118.

Dvr Voy Certin

Place	Date	Hour	Summary of Events and Information	Remarks and references to Appendices
CUCQ	28.9.14	Routine		
"	29.9.14	Routine		
"	30.9.14	Routine	Escorted 32 Civil Nurses by rail to NEUFCHATEL	
"	1.10.14	Routine	Ptes Lewis & Smith attached for duty with 11 civilian Nurses suffering from Mange at AIRON ST VAAST.	

APP. A

Officer Commanding,
    Royal Horse Guards,   20th M.V.S.
    10th Royal Hussars,   Supply Officer,
    Essex Yeomanry,   Transport Officer,
    8th Machine Gun Squadron, A.D.C.
    'G' Battery, R.H.A.   O.C. Signals,
    8th C.F.A.   6th Cavalry Brigade.

                                              B.M. 228/6.

1.   Units will march independantly to new billets as per table attached on 22nd inst.,

2.   Squadrons and Detachments woll take 200 yards distance and march as nearly as possible at 6 m.p.h.

3. (a) A. Echelons will accompany units.

   (b) B Echelons will march independantly to new areas.

         That of Royal Horse Guards to clear main HESDIN – MONTREUIL road directly in rear of regiment.
         Of 10th Hussars and Essex Yeomanry as soon as tail of Essex Yeomanry is clear of MARESQUEL.
         Of M.G.S., C.F.A, M.V.S., as soon as G Battery is clear of main road.

4.   Units will leave behind a party under an Officer to clear up billets, in case of regiments, 1 Officer per squadron.

5.   Formed parties of 6th Brigade with led horses must be given preference on the road.

6.   No troops will pass through MONTREUIL.

                                        S Hardy
21/12/16.   Capt,
                             Brigade Major, 8th Cavalry Brigade.

Unit in order of march.	Route
Royal Horse Guards,	BOIS JEAN – WAILLY.
10th Royal Hussars	LA NEUVILLE, BOIS JEAN, BAHOT., RANG DU FLIERS.
Essex Yeomanry.	LA NEUVILLE, and by any routes after passing church BOIS JEAN.
?th Machine Gun Squadron.	BOIS JEAN, BAHOT.
'G' Battery. R.H.A.	RUINE LE SEC.
?th C.F.A.	Optional.
?0th M.V.S.	"
?rals, Supplies & ?rigade Headquarters,	"

WAR DIARY
or
INTELLIGENCE SUMMARY.   20 Mot Vety Sec

(Erase heading not required.)

Army Form C. 2118.

Vol 2 3

Place	Date	Hour	Summary of Events and Information	Remarks and references to Appendices
COCQ	1.1.19	—	Routine	
"	2.1.19		15 Horses evacuated by road to 13 Vety Hospital NEUCHATEL	
"	3.1.19		Routine	
"	4.1.19		Routine	
"	5.1.19		Evacuated two horses by road to 13 Vety Hospital NEUCHATEL	
"	6.1.19		Pte LEWIS & Pte NUTTER returned to Section from AIRON ST VAAST	
"	7.1.19		Routine	
"	8.1.19		Routine	
"	9.1.19		Routine	
"	10.1.19		Routine	
"	11.1.19		Manifested stated received by horses suffering from mange of 3rd Dragoon Guards at AIRON NOTRE DAME	
"	12.1.19		Routine	
"	13.1.19		Routine – 11 horses evacuated by road to 13 Vety Hospital NEUCHATEL	
"	14.1.19		Routine	
"	15.1.19		Routine	

WAR DIARY
or
INTELLIGENCE SUMMARY.   To Mrs Petty Rector
(Erase heading not required.)

Army Form C. 2118.

Instructions regarding War Diaries and Intelligence Summaries are contained in F. S. Regs., Part II. and the Staff Manual respectively. Title pages will be prepared in manuscript.

Place	Date	Hour	Summary of Events and Information	Remarks and references to Appendices
CCCQ	16.1.19	Routine	SE2144 Col/QCpl WILLIAMS reported for duty from No 2 Vety Hospital	
"	17.1.19	Routine	SE14.610 Cpl/QCpl MESSER struck off from No 2 Vety Hospital	
"	18.1.19	Routine		
"	19.1.19	Routine		
"	20.1.19	Routine	2 Horses evacuated by road to 13 Vety Hospital NEUFCHATEL	
"	21.1.19	Routine		
"	22.1.19	Routine		
"	23.1.19	Routine		
"	24.1.19	Routine		
"	25.1.19	Routine	2 Horses evacuated by road to 13 Vety Hospital NEUFCHATEL	
"	26.1.19	Routine		
"	27.1.19	Routine		
"	28.1.19	Routine		
"	29.1.19	Routine		
"	30.1.19	Routine		
"	31.1.19	Routine	1 Horse evacuated by road to 13 Vety Hospital NEUFCHATEL	

Army Form C. 2118.

WAR DIARY
or
INTELLIGENCE SUMMARY. 20 Mot. Vety. Extn.

Vol 2

(Erase heading not required.)

Instructions regarding War Diaries and Intelligence Summaries are contained in F.S. Regs., Part II. and the Staff Manual respectively. Title pages will be prepared in manuscript.

Place	Date	Hour	Summary of Events and Information	Remarks and references to Appendices
CUCQ	1.2.19	9.a.m	Moved off with the unit as per new billets at PLANQUES — Transport following in charge of Pte TEBB — itinerary over 9 roads very slippery — getting worse during the day — Route St JOSSE, SORRUS, ECOIRES, BEAUMERIE, BRIMEUX, MARESQUEL, AUBIN St VAAST, GAYRON, WAMBERCOURT, FRESSIN.	APP. A.
PLANQUES		2 p.m.	PLANQUES. 2 horses unable to get further and the men by night very fatigued. Arrived in new billets with the right half of section. Transport owing to bad state of the road could only make very slow progress — Horse in front kicked at the lightest incline & had to be assisted up by the limber horses. Transport did not arrive until 2.30 a.m. the following morning.	CO
"	2.2.19		Arranging horse lines in the new billets.	CO
"	3.2.19		Dental — Received orders that no horse to be evacuated until further orders	CO
"	4.2.19		Routine	CO
"	5.2.19		Routine	CO
"	6.2.19		Routine	CO
"	7.2.19		Routine	CO

Army Form C. 2118.

WAR DIARY
or
INTELLIGENCE SUMMARY. 20 Mt. Vety. Section.
(Erase heading not required.)

Instructions regarding War Diaries and Intelligence Summaries are contained in F. S. Regs., Part II. and the Staff Manual respectively. Title pages will be prepared in manuscript.

Place	Date	Hour	Summary of Events and Information	Remarks and references to Appendices
PLANQUES	8.2.14	—	Routine.	
"	9.2.14		Routine.	
"	10.2.14		Routine.	
"	11.2.14		Routine.	
"	12.2.14		Routine.	
"	13.2.14		Routine — 14443 Pte HALL G 9th Bn Yorkshire Regt joined from 3 Field Ambce P.B.mn.IV	
"	14.2.14		Routine. SE2980 Pte CROSS I evacuated with 25 Gen Ho.	
"	15.2.14		Routine.	
"	16.2.14		Routine.	
"	17.2.14		Routine.	
"	18.2.14		Routine.	
"	19.2.14		Routine.	
"	20.2.14		Routine. SE8091 Pte GLASGOW W joined from No 4 Vety Ho.	
"	21.2.14		Routine.	
"	22.2.14		Routine.	
"	23.2.14		Routine. 14443 Pte HALL G 9th Bn Yorkshire Regt ordered to join his Base Depot	

WAR DIARY
or
INTELLIGENCE SUMMARY. 20 M.T. Vety Section.

(Erase heading not required.)

Army Form C. 2118.

Instructions regarding War Diaries and Intelligence Summaries are contained in F. S. Regs., Part II. and the Staff Manual respectively. Title pages will be prepared in manuscript.

Place	Date	Hour	Summary of Events and Information	Remarks and references to Appendices
PLANQUES	24.2.17		Routine	
	25.2.17		Routine	
	26.2.17		Routine	
	27.2.17		Routine	
	28.2.17		Routine. 2 Mules evacuated to 14 Art Vety Sec. for 13 10a Hos by road	

APP. A

Officer Commanding,
Royal Horse Guards,   — 20th M.V.S.
10th Royal Hussars,   Supply Officer,
Essex Yeomanry,   O.C. Signal Troop.
8th Machine Gun Squadron,   Transport Officer.
8th C.F.A.   3rd Cav.Div'n.)
A.D.C.   7th Cav.Bde.) For information.

B.M. 229/A.

1. Units will march independantly to the new area on Thursday 1st prox, as per table attached.

2. a Squadrons and detachments will take g200 yards distance and march as nearly as possible at 5 m.p.h.

   b. Horsed parties of the 7th Brigade with led horses must be given preference on the road by everyone.

3. a 'A' Echelons will accompany their units.

   b. 'B' Echelons will march independantly under a responsible N.C.O., to be detailed by each unit.

4.   Units must leave behind a party under an Officer to see billets handed over in good order, in case of regiments, one Officer per Squadron.

28/1/17.   Capt,
                        Brigade Major, 8th Cavalry Brigade.

MARCH TABLE.

Unit in order of march.	Starting point.	Time.	Route.	Billeting area.	Remarks.
Royal Horse Guards.	X roads at 1st A of ARTESIAN VILLE.	9 a.m. or earlier.	WAILLY – BOIS JEAN – J of ST.DENIS – BEAURAINVILLE – CAMBY.	PREMES – COUPELLE NEUVE – COUPELLE VILLE.	To be clear of BOIS JEAN by 10 a.m. - N of BEAURAINVILLE by 11.45 a.m. Not skirt BEAURAINVILLE by W.esterly road. GUSPLIERS sqdn to join column at BEAUCAMP.
9th Machine Gun Sqdn.	X roads S of SAHOAR?	9.45.	As for R.H.G.(except as to WAILLY).	EMCHY.	To be clear of S of BEAURAINVILLE.
10th Hussars.	X roads ST. AUBIN.	9.50.	S of SQ.SNS – SWAMSBIN – ST.MARTIN – BRICKUK – BUT DE HARLEM –ANIELA.	HYON – LOUISE – ESMOY – HIBBOVAL.	To be clear of E of SWAMBSIN VILLE by 12.15. Route optional for MIBBOVAL sqdn after passing BRIKNUX.
Essex Yeo.	X road roads & rie S.E. of ST.AUBIN.	9.45.	Follow X.H.H. as for BRIMEUX, thence via LESPINOY – from LESPINOY route optimal.	as FREDSIN – WAGNER CUNEY – CAVERN ST. MARTIN – SAINS les FREDSIN.	
20th M.V.S.) 8th G.F.A.)	Move at their own convenience.				
Bde.A... 8th M.T.	Under arrangements to be made by Camp Commandant.				

Instructions regarding War Diaries and Intelligence Summaries are contained in F. S. Regs., Part II. and the Staff Manual respectively. Title pages will be prepared in manuscript.

WAR DIARY
or
INTELLIGENCE SUMMARY.
(Erase heading not required.)

Army Form C. 2118.

20 Mobile Vety Section

Vol 2

Place	Date	Hour	Summary of Events and Information	Remarks and references to Appendices
PLANQUES	1.3.17		Routine	
"	2.3.17		Routine	
"	3.3.17		Routine	
"	4.3.17		Routine	
"	5.3.17		Routine	
"	6.3.17		Routine	
"	7.3.17		Routine	
"	8.3.17		Routine	
"	9.3.17		Routine. Evacuated 21 Cast & 1 Veterinary Case from BEURAINVILLE to 13 Vety. Hos.	
"	10.3.17		Routine.	
"	11.3.17		Routine	
"	12.3.17		Routine Evacuated 24 Cast horses BEAURAINVILLE to 13 Vety Hos.	
"	13.3.17		Routine	
"	14.3.17		Routine.	
"	15.3.17		Routine	
"	16.3.17		Routine.	

T2134. Wt. W708—776. 500000. 4/15. Sir J. C. & S.

WAR DIARY
or
INTELLIGENCE SUMMARY.   30 Mob. Vety. Sec.

Army Form C. 2118.

Place	Date	Hour	Summary of Events and Information	Remarks and references to Appendices
ALNOYES	17.3.17		Routine	
"	18.3.17		Routine	
"	19.3.17		Received orders to be ready to move at short notice.	APP. A.
"	20.3.17		Packed up ready to move. 3/1 Sgt. TEBB badly kicked sent to Hospital.	
"	21.3.17		Strained to Vet local catts that we probably should not move for some time.	
"	22.3.17		Received orders for evacuation.	
"	23.3.17		Evacuated 3/1 horses to 14 Mob. Vety. Sec. en route to 13 Vety. Sec. - Received message that Sn horses were unfit to travel further - Also some sick thro' Vetp Sec.	
"	24.3.17		Routine	
"	25.3.17		Routine	
"	26.3.17		Received orders for evacuation 17th unofficially that we should move 28.3.17 - 3/1 Sgt. TEBB I.W. evacuated from Division to 26 General Hospital.	
"	27.3.17		Evacuated 16 ord. ordinary cases to 14 M.V.S. en route to 13. Vety. Sec.	
"	28.3.17		Routine. Standing to.	
"	29.3.17		Routine.	
"	30.3.17		Routine.	
"	31.3.17		Routine.	

A.P.P. A.

S E C R E T.

Officer Commanding,
  Royal Horse Guards,   8th C.F.A.
  10th Royal Hussars,   Capt. Baker.
  Essex Yeomanry,   8th Signal Troop.
  8th Machine Gun Squadron.   2/Lieut Hann.
  G Battery, R.H.A.   Supplies.
    20th M.V.S.

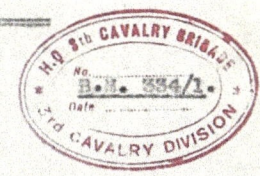

The following received from 3 Cavalry Division begins:-

"Orders have been received that a Cavalry Brigade may under certain circumstances be required to move quickly to the First Army area West of VIMY RIDGE. The 8th Cavalry Brigade is detailed and should be ready to move at 8½ hours notice. G Battery will in all probability accompany it. No further details are as yet available.
'B' Echelon will not accompany the Brigade. 'A' Echelon will be packed in accordance with my G.853 of the 3/5/17.
Units should be informed by Special D.R. and not over the wire. Acknowledge. Addressed 8th Cavalry Brigade repeated C.R.H.A. and A.A.& Q.M.G." ENDS.

Enclosed is a list of articles to be carried on 'A' Echelon wagons. In an doubtful cases the same method of carrying equipment etc should be used a s last year, and the same quantity of reserve rations etc carried.

※ Not included

Acknowledge and keep offices open all night.

The above instructions will not cancel any arrangements in force for tomorrow.

19/5/17.

                                       Capt,
                        Brigade Major, 8th Cavalry Brigade.

WAR DIARY or INTELLIGENCE SUMMARY.

20 Mtr. Vety Section.

Army Form C. 2118.

Vol 26

Place	Date	Hour	Summary of Events and Information	Remarks and references to Appendices
PLANQUES	1.4.17	—	Routine	
"	2.4.17	—	Routine	
"	3.4.17	—	This Section evacuated to 4 Mtr. Vety. Sec.	
"	4.4.17	—	Received orders to move to FRESSIN next day - FRESSIN 16 miles	
			BEAUVRAINVILLE to NEUFCHATEL	
"	5.4.17	11 a.m.	Section moved off at 11 a.m. to billets at FRESSIN.	
FRESSIN	6.4.17		Received orders that on march more following day to FREVENT area	
			— FREVENT 23 hours to NEUFCHATEL	
"	7.4.17	9 a.m.	Moved off to starting point in a snow storm via RUMENVILLE &	APP. A
		10 a.m.	Arrived the starting point at AUCHY LEZ HESDIN. Thereon via LE PARCQ	
			FRESNOY, WILLEMAN, LYNZEUX, FLERS, to FREVENT.	
FREVENT	"	4 p.m.	Arrived & bivouaced in a field horses taken in the open - No one quite	
			fine weather	
"	8.4.17		Received orders that this Mtr. Vety. Sec. were now coming under of the	
			A.D.V.S. for movements. Received orders that this Section would	
			proceed the rear of Divisional Troops to GOUY EN ARTOIS	

Army Form C. 2118.

WAR DIARY
or
INTELLIGENCE SUMMARY.
(Erase heading not required.)

20 Mot. Mty. Sec.

Place	Date	Hour	Summary of Events and Information	Remarks and references to Appendices
FREVENT	6.4.17		Requisnd horses for evacuation but on arrival found that it was only possible to evacuate sick horses on two days a week in the 3rd Army Area except under very exceptional circumstances — It is to be regretted that this information was not furnished to us beforehand. Selected the first to collect a horse unable to move from the 8th M[achine] Gun Squadron — This horse was a valuable charger — Before the field of the Section an order was received from A.D.V.S. Brillies a L.D. horse from the 3rd Div. Squadron. The Charger in consequence had to be left behind. I would ask that the officer in charge of the field should have been allowed time this association settled before moving animal.	
	2 h		Moved off from Hornoy at FREVENT going near by Amiouval through AUXIVILLE via REBREUVIETTE, LIENCOURT, AVESNES LE COMTE, FOSSEUX, to GOUY EN ARTOIS.	
GOUY EN ARTOIS		10.30pm	arrived at destination bivouaced in field with 13 & 14 Mot. Mty. Secs. Night fine & bright moonlight.	

Army Form C. 2118.

WAR DIARY
or
INTELLIGENCE SUMMARY. 20 Mtr. Vosges
(Erase heading not required.)

Place	Date	Hour	Summary of Events and Information	Remarks and references to Appendices
GOUY EN ARTOIS.	9.4.19		Starting to – Advance march Bn in direction of ARRAS – 13th, 14th Mtr. Vosges also moved towards ARRAS – nulled frosty behind & mild till hours were new viviol in by the other two Mtr Vosges for evacuation	
"	10.4.19		Routine – Received a few horses for evacuation	
"	11.4.19		Routine – SE 6604 Pte TOWNSEND N.Y. joined from Mtr Vosg. H.Q.	
"	12.4.19		Evacuated 16 horses from GOUY to ABBEVILLE. Routine – A.CO. in charge of horses refurth Pat AM and lifts not station owing to a breakdown on the line	
"	13.4.19		Received horses for evacuation –	
"	14.4.19		Evacuated 94 horses & two mules from GOUY to ABBEVILLE – this op 14,000 cash in this Section all told – Snow storm nearly all day.	
"	15.4.19		Received horses for evacuation – Lift Fost an unusual number of horses of Enquire	
"	16.4.19		Evacuated 110 horses & 22 mules from GOUY to ABBEVILLE – 8 men were away for a conducting party – these were retained by the authorities at the D.C. 10th Rly. Horses – Received orders to turn to the following day but as these were no horses to evacuate asked for permission to remain Asked for a day to evacuate the remainder	

2358 Wt. W2344/1454 700,000 5/15 D. D. & L. A.D.S.S./Forms/C. 2118.

WAR DIARY
or
INTELLIGENCE SUMMARY. 2nd/1st W.Rid.F.A.

Army Form C. 2118.

Place	Date	Hour	Summary of Events and Information	Remarks and references to Appendices
GOUY EN ARTOIS	17.4.17		Evacuated 20 horses QVK to ABBEVILLE. Brewery Horses provided by O.C. Base Remounts. Packed up ready to move off following day – Snowing.	
"	18.4.17	12 a.a.	Moved off in a Blizzard via BAVINCOURT, LAHERLIÈRE, MONDICOURT, DOULLENS, MEZEROLLES to REMAISNIL	
REMAISNIL		2.30 p.m.	Arrived in billets. Received orders from A.D.V.S. to furnish a 2000 [?] Green Remounts and 8th Div. Field Amb. It is not [?] under that [Russian?] stamp [?] the officer commanding a unit with vety. section to Commissary a Veterinary charge [?] of a regiment and another unit in the [?]. Receive orders that the Brigade would march the following day to	
			MAREJQUEL area.	
REMAISNIL	19.4.17	10 a.a.	Moved off in rear of 8th Div. Fd. Amb. to starting point. Proceeded via AUXI LECHATEAU, LABROYE, REGNAUVILLE, BRAILLY CAPELLE, LAMBUS to JUMEL.	
		5 p.m.	Arrived at JUMEL with 8th Div kind of Ration.	
JUMEL	20.4.17	9 a.a.	Sgnry Kann & [?] arrived. Rations – Rations & Men allotted – Unable to attach to the section personally. Was unable to go to Q. Ration. 8th Div. Fd. Amb.	

Army Form C. 2118.

WAR DIARY
or
INTELLIGENCE SUMMARY. 25 Mtr. V.A.D. Co.
(Erase heading not required.)

Place	Date	Hour	Summary of Events and Information	Remarks and references to Appendices
JUMEL	21.4.17		Routine.	
"	22.4.17		Routine.	
"	23.4.17		Evacuated 16 Wounded BEAUVRAINVILLE to NEUFCHATEL	
"	24.4.17		Routine.	
"	25.4.17		Evacuated 24 Wounded BEAUVRAINVILLE to NEUFCHATEL	
"	26.4.17		Routine.	
"	27.4.17		Routine.	
"	28.4.17		Evacuated 20 Wounded BEAUVRAINVILLE to NEUFCHATEL	
"	29.4.17		Routine.	
"	30.4.17		Routine.	

APP. A

Officer Commanding,
   Royal Horse Guards,   8th Signal Troop,
   10th Royal Hussars,   2nd/Lieut. HANN,
   Essex Yeomanry   2nd/Lieut. HOW,
   8th M.G.S.,   Captain E.V. BAKER,
   "O" Battery. R.H.A.   Staff Captain,
   8th C.F.A.,   A.D.C.
   20th M.V.S.,   Supply Officer.

                                                   B.M. N74.

The Brigade will march as follows tomorrow 7th inst:-

1. (a) <u>Starting Point.</u> AUCHY-lez-HESDIN Station. 10 a.m.
   (b) <u>Order of March.</u> R.H.Gds., E.Y., X.R.H., 8th M.G.S., "O" Battery, 8th C.F.A., 20th M.V.S., "A" Echelon, "B" Echelon and A.H.T.
   (c) <u>Route.</u> LE PARCQ - FRESNOY - WILLEMAN - LINZEUX - FLERS - HAUTE COTE.
   (d) <u>Billets.</u> PREVENT - LIGNY-sur-CANCHE.

2. (a) Units will assemble as under :-

      R.H.Gds.   ...   Head at S.P. tail towards WAMIN.
      E.Y.   ...   In rear of R.H.Gds.,
      X.R.H.   ...   In rear of E.Y.,
      M.G.S.   ...   In rear of X.R.H.,
      "O" Battery,   In rear of M.G.S.,
      8th C.F.A. and 20th M.V.S. (marching via BEAUVILLE will *not* come into the WAMIN - AUCHY-les-HESDIN Station till tail of M.G.Sqdn. is clear.
   (b) After passing S.P. a distance of 500 yards will be maintained between Regiments, M.G.Sqdn., and Battery.

3. (a) "A" Echelon will be brigaded as usual on passing the starting point under 2nd/Lieut HANN.
   (b) "B" Echelon and A.H.T. will march independantly in rear of Units to the Starting Point where they will be brigaded at 11 a.m. under Captain BAKER.
Follow the Brigade in the same order of march as above.
They must give road preference to other troops on their way to Starting Point.
   (c) Units will arrange to divert their Echelons at HAUTE COTE of necessary.

4. All cyclists will rendezvous at S.P. at 9-50 a.m. and march independantly under Senior Armourer.

5. On leaving the PREVENT area on the 8th inst, all "B" Echelon and A.H.T. will be deivisionalized and concentrate at BOUBERS -sur-CANCHE under orders of O.C., A.S.C.

6. Divisional Headquarters will be at MONCHEL.

                                 (Sgd) G.J. HARDY, Captain,
                             Brigade Major, 8th Cavalry Brigade.

6/4/17.

<u>Copies 1 to 15 as per Standing Orders.</u>

WAR DIARY
or
INTELLIGENCE SUMMARY. No. Mt. Vety. Sec.

Army Form C. 2118.

Vol 27

Place	Date	Hour	Summary of Events and Information	Remarks and references to Appendices
JUMEL	1.5.19		Routine.	
"	2.5.19		Routine.	
"	3.5.19		Routine.	
"	4.5.19		Routine.	
"	5.5.19		Routine.	
"	6.5.19		Routine.	
"	7.5.19		Routine.	
"	8.5.19		Routine.	
"	9.5.19		Routine.	
"	10.5.19		Routine. — 38 horses evacuated BEAVRAINVILLE to 13 Vety. Sec.	
"	11.5.19		Routine. 11 horses evacuated BEAVRAINVILLE to 13 Vety. Sec.	
"	12.5.19		Packing up ready for move — 20 horses evacuated BEAVRAINVILLE to 13 Vety. AHO.	
"	13.5.19	9.0 am	Moved off to starting point via CAMPAGNE LEZ HESDIN — LAMBUS.	APP. A.
		11.35am	Passed starting point proceeded in rear of 8th Cav Fd Amb. via CHERIENNE FONTAINE L'ETALON to VAULX.	
		4 P.M.	Arrived at VAULX billetted in & field — Thunderstorm during night SE6462 Pte HAWTIN. F admitted to Hospital evacuated.	

WAR DIARY or INTELLIGENCE SUMMARY

Army Form C. 2118.

To Mr. Vary Co.

Place	Date	Hour	Summary of Events and Information	Remarks and references to Appendices
VAULX	14.5.17	11 a.m.	Moved off in rear of 8th Can. Fd. Amb. to starting point – Heard that our squadron of 10th Roy. Hussars had stampeded during the storm and horses circulars only sights – Marched via AUXI LE CHATEAU WAVENS to FROHEN LE GRAND	APP. B.
FROHEN LE GRAND		1 p.m.	Arrived at destination & horsed in a very wet & windy field – Rained very hard for the rest of the day – Billed two horses at CANDAS & informed V.O.s that my mules carried horses the following day if any cases were received – No horses sent in.	
"	15.5.17	8 a.m.	Moved off to starting point in rear of 8th Can. Fd. Amb. & proceeded via GEZAIN COURT BEAUVAL LA VICOGNE to TALMAS.	APP. C.
TALMAS	15.5.17	3 p.m.	Arrived at destination & billeted in squares – No horses for evacuation	
"	16.5.17	9.15 a.m.	Moved off in rear of 8th Can. Fd. Amb. to starting point & proceeded via MOLLIENS AU BOIS to QUERRIEU. – Billeted horses own in thorough field Remounts Depot.	APP. D.
QUERRIEU	16.5.17	1 p.m.	Arrived in Billets.	
"	17.5.17	10 a.m.	Moved off to starting point & proceeded via DAOURS. FOUILLOY- HAMELET to HAMEL	APP. E.

WAR DIARY
or
INTELLIGENCE SUMMARY.
(Erase heading not required.)

Army Form C. 2118.

20 Mbile Vety Section

Place	Date	Hour	Summary of Events and Information	Remarks and references to Appendices
HAMEL	15.5.19	2 P.M.	Arrived in billets — Very dirty & unsanitary and approximately 3 kilometres from a watering place for horses.	
"	16.5.19		Remained in billets cleaning saddlery	
"	19.5.19	8 A.M.	Moved off to watering place on the way to starting point.	
		9.30 A.M.	Passed starting point & proceeded via MERICOURT CHUIGNOLLES CHUIGNES DOMPIERRE HERBECOURT BIACHES PERONNE DOINGT COURCELLES	
HERBECOURT		12.30 P.M.	Off saddled and grazed horses for one hour	APPF
COURCELLES		4 P.M.	Arrived at destination & bivouaced in an orchard	
"	20.5.19		Cleaning saddlery.	OK
"	21.5.19		Routine.	OK
"	22.5.19		Routine — Evacuated Tem Nuevo PERONNE to M.V. Vety. Sn.	OK
"	23.5.19		Routine.	OK
"	24.5.19		Routine. T34408 Dr GRIMES A.A. & T32361 Dr LEWIS E. reported for duty	OK
"	25.5.19		Routine.	
"	26.5.19		Routine. Evacuated 3 horses TINCOURT to M.V. Vety. Sn.	OK

WAR DIARY
or
INTELLIGENCE SUMMARY.

20 Mob. Vety. Sec.

Army Form C. 2118.

Place	Date	Hour	Summary of Events and Information	Remarks and references to Appendices
COURCELLES	27.5.17		Routine.	
"	28.5.17		Routine. SE 4890 PTE LIVIE G. evacuated patient for No 1 Vety. Hos.	AV AV AV AV AV
"	29.5.17		Routine.	
"	30.5.17		Routine.	
"	31.5.17		Routine.	

APP. A

[Stamp: H.Q. 8 CAVALRY BRIGADE / 3rd CAVALRY DIVISION]

Royal Horse Guards,　　　　　　20th M.V.S.
10th Royal Hussars,　　　　　　 8th Signal Troop.
Essex Yeomanry,　　　　　　　　Camp Commandant.
G. Battery, R.H.A.　　　　　　 Capt. Baker, A.S.C.
8th M.G.S.　　　　　　　　　　 Supply Officer,
8th C.F.A.　　　　　　　　　　　O.C., Brigade cyclists.

Ref. Map. 1/100,000. Abbeville & Lens.　　　B.M. 87/7.

1. The Brigade, less Essex Yeomanry, will march tomorrow 19th inst in accordance with attached march table. After passing the starting point units will march independantly.
   On 19th inst the Brigade will march to an area between FROHEN LE GRAND and REN.

2. Essex Yeomanry will march independantly of the rest of the Brigade. They will follow the tail of the 6th Cav. Bde along N. bank of River AUTHIE through GOUNIEZ and LABROYE.
   They will not pass LABROYE till 11.20 a.m. and will be clear of it by 11.50 a.m. They will billet at GUEUX-IVERGNY and VILLERY.

3. Units of the 6th Cav. Bde will not cross to the N. of R. AUTHIE until the tail of Divisional Troops has passed.

4. A distance of 800 yards will be maintained in rear of each Regiment, Battery and M.G.Sqdn.

5. "A" Echelons will march in rear of Units under an Officer to be detailed by each.

6. "B" Echelon will march to the starting point independantly where they will come under the orders of Capt. Baker, A.S.C. at 12 noon. They will pass the starting point in order of march of units, and Capt. Baker will arrange for them to proceed by the same route as their units.

7. All Brigade cyclists will be at the Starting Point at 10.45 a.m. where they will come under the orders of 2/Lieut. HUGHES, 10th Royal Hussars.

8. On arrival in new billeting area Brigade Headquarters will be at VAULX.

9. Acknowledge.

18/8/17.　　　　　　　　　　　　　　　　La Fielden
　　　　　　　　　　　　　　　　　　　　　　　　Capt.
　　　　　　　　　　　　　　　Brigade Major, 8th Cavalry Brigade.

MARCH TABLE.

Unit.	Starting point.	Time.	Route.	Billeting area.	Remarks.
Bde H.Q.	Cross roads 1175 yards 130° G. of Y of MAYVILLE.	11 a.m.	First R. of MOREUIL - GUYOT - DEMUIN - FONTAINE L'EVEQUE 1 of GENNES-IGNAUX.	VAUX.	
8th C.Y.	"	11 a.m.	"	"	
10th Hussars.	"	11 a.m.		LA FORESTE - VIT-VILLIERS - HOUTTAKES.	
S.E.Bde.	"	11.10 a.m.	Main ARMENTIÈRE road.	LE SOIGH.	1. Not to pass LARMUS till tail of T.M.B. is clear. 2. Not to pass LARMUTS till 11.30 when E/Bec should be clear.
8th S.L.B.	"	11.20 a.m.	Same as Bde. H.Q.	WILLENCOURT - LA FRESVILLE.	Be clear of road to starting Point till tail of T.M.Bde has passed.
G.Sty. L.S.A.	"	11.25 a.m.	Main ARMENTIÈRE road.	LARMUTS.	Not to pass LARMUS till tail of T.M.Bde is clear.
8th C.F.A.	"	11.30 a.m.	Same as Bde H.Q.	VAUX.	Stands clear of main ARMENTIÈRE road till tail of G. Battery has passed.
20th A.L.B.	"	11.30 a.m.	Same as Bde H.Q.	VAUX.	

APP. B

Royal Horse Guards,   Capt. Baker, A.S.C.
10th Royal Hussars,   Capt. Harford, R.H.A.
Essex Yeomanry,   Staff Captain,
G. Battery, R.H.A.   2/Lieut. Hughes, K.R.H. 1/c Bde
8th M.G.Sqdn.   Cyclists).
8th C.F.A.
20th M.V.S.   Supply Officer,
8th Signal Troop.   3rd Cav. Divn. (For information).

Ref. Map 1/100,000. LENS.   B.M. 45.

1. The Brigade will march tomorrow 14th inst to a billeting area HEM - OCCOCHES - OUTREBOIS - MEZEROLLES - FROHEN-LE-GRAND - FROHEN-LE-PETIT.
   REMAISNIL - BARLY - BOIS BERGUES and HARDINVAL are available if required.

2. The Brigade will march in two columns as under:-

   (a) **Column X** under command of Lieut.Col. F.H. WHITMORE, D.S.O., Essex Yeomanry.

   (b) **Starting Point.** Cross-roads just N. of A of LA NEUVILLE.

   (c) **Route.** Road N. of R. AUTHIE - AUXI-LE-CHATEAU - WAVENS - FROHEN-LE-GRAND.

   (d) **Order Of March.** Time of passing   Remarks.
                            Starting Point.
   Brigade Headquarters.   11-20 a.m.
   8th Signal Troop.   11-20 a.m.
   Essex Yeomanry.   11-20 a.m.
   "G" Battery, R.H.A.   11-30 a.m.
   8th C.F.A.   11-35 a.m.
   20th M.V.S.   11-40 a.m.

   (e) "B" Echelons of this column will march independently in rear of units to the Starting Point where they will come under Captain BAKER, A.S.C. They will pass the Starting Point at 12 Noon in order of march as Units.

3. (a) **Column Y.** under command of Lieut-Col. LORD TWEEDMOUTH, M.V.O., Royal Horse Guards.   CMG DSO.

   (b) **Starting Point.** cross roads just E. of T of WILLENCOURT.

   (c) **Route.** Road S. of R. AUTHIE - AUXI-LE-CHATEAU - BEAUVOIR - RIVIERE - ~~KNEMOGRNESHUDNE~~ - FROHEN-LE-PETIT.

   (d) **Order of March.** Time of passing   Remarks.
                            Starting Point.
   Royal Horse Guards   11-30 a.m.
   10th Royal Hussars.   11-40 a.m.   Must not block the road
                                          at LE PONCHEL for
                                          Column X.
   8th M.G.S.   11-50 a.m.

- 2 -

N.B. (a) In passing through AUXI-LE-CHATEAU this column must keep to the S. bank of the R.AUTHIE.

(b) On arriving in billeting area units of this column will give way to units of column K when moving to N. bank of R. AUTHIE.

(c) B. Echelons of this column will march to the starting point independently where they will come under the orders of Capt. Burford, R.H.G. They will pass the starting point at 12.15 p.m. in order of march of units.

4. 'A' Echelons of both columns will march in rear of units under an officer to be detailed by each.

5. A distance of 300 yards will be maintained in rear of each regiment, battery and M.G.Sqdn.

6. All brigade cyclists will be at the starting point of Column X. at 11.15 a.m. where they will come under the orders of 2/Lieut. Hughes, R.E.D.

7. On arrival in new billeting area Brigade Headquarters will be at FROHEN-LE-GRAND.

                                                       Capt.

15/5/17.   Brigade Major, 8th Cavalry Bde.

Allotment of billets in new area is attached.

Copies as per orders.

Billets have been allotted for Billeting Area 14/8/17 as follows:-

Brigade Headquarters, 8th C.F.A. 20th H.V.A.	FROMEN-LE-GRAND.
Royal Horse Guards,	COCOCHES.
10th Royal Hussars	MAKENOLLES - OUTRE BOIS.
Essex Yeomanry.	HAMLN.
"U" Battery, R.H.A.	HEM.
8th M.G.Squadron.	FROMEN-LE-PETIT.

15/8/17.

R. Fielden Capt,
Brigade Major, 8th Cavalry Brigade.

APP. C

Royal Horse Guards,   20th H.V.S.
10th Royal Hussars,   9th Signal Troop,
Essex Yeomanry,   Staff Captain,
C. Battery, R.H.A.   Capt. Baker, A.S.C.
9th Machine Gun Sqdn.   Supply Officer
9th C.F.A.   3rd Cav. Div. (for information)

Ref. No. 1/100.023. A.Q.

1. The Brigade will march tomorrow 15th inst by 3 roads to a new billeting area TALMAS – RAVENEAS – CANDIEUS – NAOURS.
   The Brigade will not enter new billeting area before 11 a.m.

2. After passing starting point units may march independently but should maintain liason with units in rear and inform them when they intend halting etc.,
   A distance of at least 300 yards will be maintained in rear of each Regiment, Battery and M.G.Sqdn.

3. "A" Echelons will march in rear of units under an officer to be detailed by each.

4. "B" Echelons will march independantly by the same routes as their unit, under an officer to be detailed by each unit.
   "B" Echelons must give way to fighting troops.

5. Cyclists will march independently by the same routes as units in front of each column under an N.C.O. to be detailed by each unit.

6. The Staff Captain will meet billeting parties as follows:-

   Representatives of Royal Horse Guards, 9th C.F.A., 9th M.G. 9th Signal Troop, 20th H.V.S., at the
   Town Majors office, TALMAS at 10.15 a.m.

   Representatives of 10th Hussars and "C" Battery, R.H.A. at
   Town Majors office, NAOURS at 9.45 a.m.

7. Brigade Headquarters will be at TALMAS on arrival in new billeting area.

14/5/17.   Capt.
                                   Brigade Major, 8TH Cavalry Brigade.

Issued at 4.15pm.

Unit.	Starting Point.	Time.	Route.	Billeting Area.	Remarks.
Bde. H.Qrs. 8th Sig.Sub.	Eastern exit of HEM.	9.55 a.m.	GUZAINCOURT – BERTVAL – LA VICOGNE.	TALMAS.	
R.H.Q.	Eastern exit of HEM.	8. a.m.	GUZAINCOURT – BERTVAL – LA VICOGNE.	TALMAS.	
L.R.H.	LN of LE CHEPEL FARM.	9. a.m.	PIERVILLERS – CANAPLES.	HALONS.	
B.Vet.	LN of LE CHEPEL FARM.	9.15 a.m.	Same as R.H.Q.	HAVERNAS.	Will drop way at OUTREBOIS to Bde H.Q. 5th C.F.A. & 20th B.V.C. marching along N. bank of river.
"J" Bty.	Eastern exit of HEM.	9.10 a.m.	GUZAINCOURT – NAIVAL.	HALONS.	Nowsin clear of road through HEM till tail of L.R.H. has passed.
5th B.C.O.	S. exit of JUNES LE GRAND.	9. a.m.	BERNAVILLE – CANAPLES.	WARURINS.	Give way to L.R.H. and B.Vet at CANAPLES Station.
5th C.F.A.	Eastern exit of HEM.	9.25 a.m.	Same as R.H.Q.	TALMAS.	
20th B.V.C.	Eastern exit of HEM	9.30 a.m.	Same as R.H.Q.	TALMAS.	Follow 5th C.F.A.

APP D.

Royal Horse Guards,	8th Signal Troop.
10th Royal Hussars,	Staff Capt.
Essex Yeomanry,	Capt. Baker, A.S.C.
'G' Battery, R.H.A.	Supply Officer,
8th Machine Gun Sqdn.	2/Lieut. Hughes, X.R.H. Bde.Cyclist
8th C.F.A.	3rd Cav. Divn. (For information).
20th M.V.S.	

Ref. Map. 1/100,000, LENS & AMIENS.

B.M. 48.

1. The Brigade will march tomorrow 16th inst to a billeting area ALLONVILLE - MOLLIENS AU BOIS - ST. GRATIEN - PONT NOYELLES - part of QUERRIEU, in accordance with attached march table.

2. 'A' Echelons will march in rear of units under an officer to be detailed by each unit.

3. 'B' Echelons will march to the Starting Point independantly where they will come under the orders of Capt. Baker, A.S.C.
   They will pass the Starting Point in order of march of units at 10.15 a.m.

4. All Brigade cyclists will be at Starting Point at 8.55 a.m. where they will come under the orders of 2/Lieut. Hughes, 10th Royal Hussars.

5. After passing the Starting Point a distance of 500 yards will be maintained in rear of each Regiment, Battery and M.G.Sqdn.

6. Allotment of billets in new area will be forwarded later.

15/5/17.

Capt,
Brigade Major, 8th Cavalry Brigade.

Issued at......

MARCH TABLE.
-:-:-:-:-:-:-:-:-:-:-:-:-

Starting Point - 6 road junction N.W. of VILLERS BOCAGE,
1 mile E. of last S of FLESSELLES.

Route.- MOLLIENS AU BOIS.

Order of march.	Time.	Remarks.
Brigade H.Q.	9 a.m.	
8th Signal Troop.	9 a.m.	
10th. Rl Hussars.	9 a.m.	Route to S.P. via FLESSELLES.
Essex Yeomanry.	9.10 a.m.	Not to pass cross roads in FLESSELLES till tail of X.R.H. is clear.
Royal Horse Gds.	9.20 a.m.	
8th M.G.Sqdn.	9.30 a.m.	Not to pass cross roads in FLESSELLES till tail of Essex Yeomanry in clear.
'G' Battery, R.H.A.	9.35 a.m.	Not to block 8th M.G.S. in NAOURS.
8th C.F.A.	9.40 a.m.	
20th M.V.S.	9.45 a.m.	

-:-:-:-:-:-:-:-:-:-:-:-:-:-:-

APP. E

Royal Horse Guards,   8th Signal Troop,
10th Royal Hussars,   Staff Captain,
Essex Yeomanry,   Capt. Baker, A.S.C.
'G' Battery, R.H.A.   Supply Officer,
8th Machine Gun Squadron.   2/Lt. Hughes, E.R.H.
8th C.F.A.   (Brigade Cyclists),
20th M.V.S.   3rd Cav. Div. (For information).

Ref. Map 1/100,000 ATTACHED.

1.   The Brigade will march tomorrow the 17th inst. to a bivouac area at HAMEL in accordance with attached march table.
    The Brigade will halt on the 18th inst. and will move into final area on the 19th inst. under orders to be issued later.

2.   'A' Echelons will march in rear of Units under an Officer to be detailed by each Unit.

3.   'B' Echelons will march to the Starting Point independantly where they will come under the orders of Captain BAKER, A.S.C.
    They will pass the Starting Point in order of march of Units at 11-15 a.m.

4.   All Brigade Cyclists will be at the Starting Point at 9-35 a.m. when they will come under the orders of 2/Lieut. HUGHES, E.R.H.

5.   After passing the Starting Point a distance of 500 yards will be maintained in rear of each Regiment, Battery and Machine Gun Squadron.

6.   The Staff Captain will meet representatives from each Unit at HAMEL Church at 10 a.m. to allot bivouac areas.

                                                  Captain,

16/6/17.   Brigade Major, 8th Cavalry Brigade.

Issued at ....

M.A.R.C.H TABLE.

Starting Point - X road junction 600x South of P. of PONT NOYELLES.

Route - DAOURS - FOUILLOY - HAMELET.

Order of march.	Time.	Remarks.
Brigade H.Q & 8th Sig: Troop.	9.40 a.m.	
Essex Yeomanry.	9.40 a.m.	
Royal Horse Guards.	9.55 a.m.	Follow Essex Yeomanry through QUERRIEU.
10th Royal Hussars.	10.10 a.m.	Not to block E.Y. and R.H.G. in PONT NOYELLES.
8th Machine Gun Sqdn.	10.25 a.m.	
'O' Battery, R.H.A.	10.35 a.m.	Follow 8th M.G.S. to S.P.
8th C.F.A.	10.45 a.m.	
20th M.V.S.	10.50 a.m.	

APP. F

Royal Horse Guards,　　　　8th Signal Troop,
10th Royal Hussars,　　　　Staff Captain,
Essex Yeomanry,　　　　　　 2nd Lt. W.R.Druce, X.R.H., i/c B.Echelon.
'G' Battery, R.H.A.　　　　Supply Officer,
8th M.G.Squadron,　　　　　2/Lt. L.V.Hughes, X.R.H. i/c
8th C.F.A.　　　　　　　　　　Brigade cyclists.
20th M.V.S.　　　　　　　　　 3rd Cav. Divn. (For information).

Ref. Map. AMIENS 1/100,000 and
1/40,000 62G.

B.M. 58.

1. The Brigade will march tomorrow 19th inst to a bivouac area J.32.B. and J.33.A., S.W. of BUIRE.

2. The Brigade, including 'B' Echelon, will be clear of DOMPIERRE by 12.30 p.m.

3. 'A' Echelons will march in rear of units under an officer to be detailed by each unit.

4. 'B' Echelons will move independantly to cross roads 1000^x W. of G of CERISY GAILLY where they will come under the orders of 2nd Lieut. Druce, X.R.H. at 9.15 a.m. They will park by the side of the road. They will pass the Starting Point in order of march of units at 9.35 a.m.

5. All Brigade Cyclists will be at the Starting Point at 8.40 a.m. when they will come under the orders of 2/Lieut. Hughes, X.R.H.

6. After passing the Starting Point a distance of 500^x will be maintained in rear of each Regiment, Battery and M.G.Sqdn.

7. Units will water before arriving at the Starting Point as laid down in Col. 4 of attached March Table.
Care will be taken not to block the unit in front when leaving present bivouac area. 'B' Echelons will water independantly before marching from HAMEL.

8. The Brigade will halt and water short of the bridge at PERONNE on arrival of the head of the column short of the bridge. Each unit will send a representative to the head of the column to receive instructions for watering etc.

9. Essex Yeomanry will detail one officer to assist the traffic control post at the bridge at PERONNE. This officer will report at 7.15 p.m. this evening at Brigade H.Q. to receive his instructions.

10. The Staff Captain will meet representatives from each unit at the cross roads just S. of LL of COURCELLES at 1 p.m.

11. Brigade Headquarters will be at COURCELLES.

R. Fielden
Capt,
Brigade Major, 8th Cavalry Brigade.

18/6/17.

4.45/pm
Issued at......

MARCH TABLE - 19.8.17.

Route - HENICOURT - CHUIGNOLLES - CHUI-NES - DOMPIERRE - HERBECOURT - BIACHES - ETINEHEM - POMMY - CHIPILLY.

Order of march.	Time.	Starting Point.	Remarks - To water at the following places before reaching Starting Point.
	Brigade.		
Brigade H.Q. 8th Signal Troop. Royal Horse Guards.	8.45 a.m. 8.45 a.m. 8.45 a.m.	Cross roads just S. of CERISY-GAILLY church.	CERISY-GAILLY.
10th Royal Hussars.	8.55 a.m.	do.	Lock S. of SAILLY LAURETTE.
Essex Yeomanry.	9.5 a.m.	do.	Point about 1000 Y. of L of NAME.
8th M.G.Sqdn.	9.15 a.m.	do.	BOUZENCOURT.
"G" Battery, R.H.A.	9.20 a.m.	do.	BOUZENCOURT.
8th C.F.A.	9.25 a.m.	do.	BOUZENCOURT.
20th M.V.S.	9.30 a.m.	do.	BOUZENCOURT.

WAR DIARY
or
INTELLIGENCE SUMMARY. 20 Mobile Vety Section
(Erase heading not required.)

Army Form C. 2118.

Vol 28

Place	Date	Hour	Summary of Events and Information	Remarks and references to Appendices
COURCELLES	1.6.17		Routine	
"	2.6.17		Routine. Evacuated 18 horses to No 7 Vety Hospital from TINCOURT	
"	3.6.17		Routine	
"	4.6.17		Routine	
"	5.6.17		Routine. Evacuated 24 horses TINCOURT to No 7 Vety Hospital	
"	6.6.17		Routine	
"	7.6.17		Routine	
"	8.6.17		Routine	
"	9.6.17		Routine. Evacuated 4 horses TINCOURT to No 7 Vety Hospital	
"	10.6.17		Routine	
"	11.6.17		Routine	
"	12.6.17		Routine. Evacuated 16 horses to No 7 Vety Hospital from TINCOURT	
"	13.6.17		Routine	
"	14.6.17		Routine	
"	15.6.17		Routine	
"	16.6.17		Routine	

Army Form C. 2118.

WAR DIARY
or
INTELLIGENCE SUMMARY. 20 Mobile Vety Section
(Erase heading not required.)

Instructions regarding War Diaries and Intelligence Summaries are contained in F. S. Regs., Part II. and the Staff Manual respectively. Title pages will be prepared in manuscript.

Place	Date	Hour	Summary of Events and Information	Remarks and references to Appendices
COURCELLES	17.6.17	Routine		
"	18.6.17	Routine		
"	19.6.17	Routine	Evacuated 10 horses TINCOURT to No.7 Vety Hospital	
"	20.6.17	Routine		
"	21.6.17	Routine		
"	22.6.17	Routine		
"	23.6.17	Routine	Evacuated 5 Mules TINCOURT to No.7 Vety Hospital	
"	24.6.17	Routine		
"	25.6.17	Routine		
"	26.6.17	Routine		
"	27.6.17	Routine		
"	28.6.17	Routine		
"	29.6.17	Routine		
	30.6.17	Routine	Evacuated 9 Horses & 1 Mule to No.7 Vety Hospital from TINCOURT. Received orders that we should move on July 2nd to SUZANNE area	

Army Form C. 2118.

WAR DIARY
or
INTELLIGENCE SUMMARY.
(Erase heading not required.)

26 A.W. Vet. Sec. No. 27

Instructions regarding War Diaries and Intelligence Summaries are contained in F.S. Regs., Part II. and the Staff Manual respectively. Title pages will be prepared in manuscript.

Place	Date	Hour	Summary of Events and Information	Remarks and references to Appendices
COURCELLES	1.7.17		Packing up preparing for move on following day	
	2.7.17	10.30am	Moved off in charge of Colour Sgt Dent via PERONNE, MARICOURT to SUZANNE	APP. A
SUZANNE		3pm	Arrived in bivouac	
	3.7.17	10.15	Moved off in rear of 8th Cav Fd Amb via BRAY-MORLANCOURT to HEILLY	APP. B
HEILLY		1.30pm	Arrived in bivouac - very dusty, few lying around which also covered w/t	
			a swamp making the night by a heavy thunderstorm	
	4.7.17	8.30am	Moved off to ?? front of ?orcelles via CONTAY TOUTENCOURT PUCHEVILLERS BEAUQUESNE to ORVILLE	APP. C
ORVILLE		2.30pm	Arrived in bivouac	
			Owing to the lack of transport it was necessary for 4 men to march on foot these marches	
	5.7.17	6.30am	SE21962 Pte ROLFE w.t. admitted to hospital. Moved off to starting point and proceeded to ETREE WAMIN.	APP. D
ETREE WAMIN		1pm	Arrived in bivouac	
	6.7.17	6am	Moved off to starting point & proceeded via MAIZIERES NERDOINGT BAILLEUL AUX CORNAILLES to DIEVAL	APP. E

WAR DIARY
or
INTELLIGENCE SUMMARY. 20 Mob. Vety. Sec.

(Erase heading not required.)

Army Form C. 2118.

Instructions regarding War Diaries and Intelligence Summaries are contained in F. S. Regs., Part II. and the Staff Manual respectively. Title pages will be prepared in manuscript.

Place	Date	Hour	Summary of Events and Information	Remarks and references to Appendices
DIEVAL	6.7.17	9.30 a	Arrived in Division — Final destination	
"	7.7.17		Routine	
"	8.7.17		Routine	
"	9.7.17		Routine	
"	10.7.17		Evacuated 5 horses BRUAY to 22 Vety. Hos.	
"	11.7.17		Routine	
"	12.7.17		Routine	
"	13.7.17		Routine. 6 horses BRUAY to 22 Vety Hos	
"	14.7.17		Routine	
"	15.7.17		Routine. Evacuated 4 horses Bruay to 22 Vety. Hos. — Received orders to move	
"	16.7.17		Packing up ready to move	
"	17.7.17	4.15 pm	Moved off via CAMBLAIN-CHATELAIN to FERFAY & thence via ST NIAIRE to	APPE
			AIRE & THIENNES	
THIENNES	18.7.17	10 am	Arrived in Division	
"	18.7.17		Routine	
"	19.7.17		Routine. SE 17444 Pte FOWLER reported for duty.	

WAR DIARY
or
INTELLIGENCE SUMMARY. 20 MT Vety Co

Army Form C. 2118.

(Erase heading not required.)

Place	Date	Hour	Summary of Events and Information	Remarks and references to Appendices
THIENNES	20.7.17	Routine		
"	21.7.17		Evacuated 14 Horses AIRE to 22 Vety. Hos.	
"	22.7.17	Routine		
"	23.7.17	Routine		
"	24.7.17	Routine		
"	25.7.17	Routine	12 Horses evacuated AIRE to 22 Vety. Hos.	
"	26.7.17	Routine		
"	27.7.17	Routine		
"	28.7.17	Routine		
"	29.7.17	Routine	10 Horses & 1 Mule evacuated AIRE to 22 Vety. Hos.	
"	30.7.17	Routine		
"	31.7.17	Routine		

APP A. Secret

R.H.G. (4)	Camp Comdt.	8th C.F.A.	20th M.V.S.
X.R.H. (4)	8th Sig. Tp	3rd C.D. "Q"	Bde. Cyclist
E.Y. (4)	S.O.	do. G.S.	Officer.
8th M.G.S.	B.T.O.	Staff Capt.	

B.M. 249/4.

Ref. Maps: 1/40,000, Sheet 62c.
1/100,000, AMIENS.

1. The 3rd Cavalry Division will be transferred from the Fourth Army (Cav. Corps) to First Army.

2. The 8th Cavalry Brigade, less G Battery, and dismounted men, will march, on July 2nd, to a new area in the vicinity of SUZANNE.
The march will be continued on July 3rd to HEILLY.

3. The head of the Brigade will pass the Starting Point - Cross Roads in COURCELLES, J.32c - at 9.30 a.m. No troops are to debouch on to the COURCELLES-BUIRE ROAD until the unit in front is clear of Starting Point.

4. Order of march: Brigade Headquarters, 8th Signal Troop, Royal Horse Guards, 10th Royal Hussars, Essex Yeomanry, 8th Machine Gun Squadron, 8th C.F.A., and 20th M.V.S.

5. "A" Echelons will march in rear of their respective units.

6. A distance of 500 yards will be maintained in rear of each Regiment and the Machine Gun Squadron.

7. All Cyclists of the Brigade will assemble at the Starting Point at 9.20 a.m. and march under the orders of an officer to be detailed by O.C., X.R.H.

8. O.C., Essex Yeomanry will detail an officer to report at Brigade Headquarters at the Starting Point. This officer will be required to assist in Traffic Control while the Brigade is passing through PERONNE.

9. "B" Echelon of the Brigade, in order of march of Units, including A.H.T., attached, will assemble at the Starting Point at 10.30 a.m., and march under the orders of the Brigade Transport Officer.

10. Heavy Section 8th C.F.A., will march separately under the orders of O.C., 8th C.F.A.

11. Route: PERONNE - MARICOURT - SUZANNE.

12. Dismounted men of the Brigade will remain in present camp and be concentrated under orders to be issued later. Capt. H.C.S. Combe, R.H.G., will assume command of the Brigade Dismounted Company on departure of the Brigade. Company Sergeant Major detailed by O.C., R.H.G., will report to him for orders.
Units will forward Nominal Rolls of dismounted men to O.C., Bde., Coy., before moving off.

13. Railhead will be at LA FLAQUE on July 4th.

14. Advance Parties will report to Staff Captain at Pt. 104, A.27.d.3.9. at 10.30 a.m. July 2nd.

15. Brigade Report Centre will close at COURCELLES at 9.30 a.m. and reopen at SUZANNE at the same hour.

16. Acknowledge.

30/6/17.

[signature]

Capt,
for Brigade Major, 8th Cav. Bde.

APP. B.

Royal Horse Guards,   20th M.V.S.
10th Royal Hussars,   Supply Officer,
Essex Yeomanry,   3rd Cavalry Division (for information)
8th Machine Gun Squadron,   Staff Captain,
8th C.F.A.   Camp Commandant.

Map Ref. 1/40,000 Sheet 62c   1/160,000 AMIENS.

B.M. 253/

1.   The Brigade will march tomorrow to the area HEILLY - MERICOURT - L'ABBE - TREUX.

2.   Starting Point. T roads S. by W. of SUZANNE CHURCH.

3.   The head of the Brigade will pass starting point at 9.30 a.m.

4.   Order of march, Brigade H.Qrs, 8th Signal Troop, 10th Hussars, Essex Yeomanry, Royal Horse Guards, 8th Machine Gun Squadron, 8th C.F.A., 20th M.V.S.

5.   "A" Echelons will march in rear of their respective Units.

6.   A distance of 500 yards will be maintained in rear of each Regiment and Machine Gun Squadron.

7.   All cyclists will assemble at the Starting Point at 9.20 a.m. and march Brigaded under an Officer to be detailed by O.C., Essex Yeomanry.

8.   "B" Echelon of the Brigade in order of march of Units will assemble at the Starting Point at 10.30 a.m. and march under the orders of the Brigade Transport Officer.

9.   Sick horses, in order of march of units, will march in rear of "B" Echelon under the orders of Capt. FETHERSTONHAUGH, A.V.C.

10.   Route. BRAY - MORLANCOURT.

11.   Each Unit will leave an Officers party behind. These officers will be responsible that their respective areas are left thoroughly clean. These parties will march independantly to new areas.

12.   Billeting Parties will meet the Staff Captain at TREUX CHURCH at 10.30 a.m.

13.   Brigade Report Centre will close at SUZANNE at 9.30 a.m. and reopen at HEILLY at the same hour.

2nd July, 1917.   Sd. F.W. WILSON FITZGERALD, Captain,
    for Brigade Major, 8th Cavalry Brigade.

Secret.

O.C. 20 M.V.S.
~~Supply Officer~~

AMPLIER &
~~STAPLE AUX S~~
ETREE WAMIN.

APP. C

Royal Horse Guards,   20th M.V.S.
10th Royal Hussars,   8th Signal Troop,
Essex Yeomanry,   Camp Commandant,
8th Machine Gun Squadron, Supply Officer
8th C.F.A.   Brigade Transport Officer,
          3rd Cavalry Division (For information).

B.M. 256.

Ref. Maps 1/100,000 AMIENS & LENS.

1. The Brigade will march tomorrow July 4th, to the area ORVILLE - AMPLIER - AUTHIEULE.

2. Starting Point cross roads 1000 yards N.W. of H in HEILLY.

3. The Brigade will assemble at the Starting Point at 9 a.m. as under -

    (a) Brigade H.Q. head at Starting Point, tail towards HEILLY, 8th Signal Troop in rear of Brigade H.Q., Royal Horse Guards in rear of 8th Signal Troop, 8th Machine Gun Squadron in rear of Royal Horse Guards.

    (b) Essex Yeomanry head at Starting Point, tail towards ALBERT, 10th Hussars in rear of Essex Yeomanry, 8th C.F.A. in rear of 10th Hussars.
        These Units to approach Starting Point via RIBEMONT.

4. Order of march - Brigade H.Qrs, 8th Signal Troop, Essex Yeomanry, Royal Horse Guards, 10th Hussars, 8th Machine Gun Squadron, 8th C.F.A., 20th M.V.S., "A" Echelon in order of march of units.

5. "A" Echelons will accompany Units to the Starting Point when they will be sidetracked and subsequently march Brigaded under the senior Quartermaster.

6. All cyclists will assemble at the Starting Point at 8.50 a.m. and march Brigaded under Lieut. SLIM, 10th Hussars.

7. "B" Echelons of the Brigade in order of march of Units will assemble at the Starting Point at 10 a.m. and march under the orders of the Brigade Transport Officer.

8. Sick horses in order of march of units will march in rear of "B" Echelon under Capt. Fotherstonhaugh, A.V.C.

9. Route - CONTAY - TOUTENCOURT - PUCHEVILLERS - BEAUQUESNE.

10. Billeting parties will meet Staff Captain at ORVILLE CHURCH at 10 a.m. Each party will send a guide to meet its Unit at X roads 400x S. of ORVILLE CHURCH.

11. Brigade Report Centre will close at HEILLY at 9 a.m. and reopen in new area at the same hour.

12. Acknowledge.

                                                    Capt,
3/7/17.   for Brigade Major, 8th Cavalry Brigade.

App. D

Royal Horse Guards,   20th M.V.S.
10th Royal Hussars,   8th Signal Troop,
Essex Yeomanry,   Camp Commandant,
8th Machine Gun Squadron,   Staff Captain,
8th C.F.A.   Supply Officer
Brigade Transport Officer,   3rd Cavalry Division (formation).

Map. 1/100,000 LENS.

1. The Brigade will march tomorrow July 5th on the area REBREUVIETTE – ETREE-WAMIN in accordance with march table over leaf.

2. 'A' Echelon will accompany units.

3. 'B' Echelon will assemble as under:-

   (a) Tenth Hussars, Essex Yeomanry and 8th C.F.A. at fork roads N. of LE of LE MARAIS SEC at 9.45 a.m. and march under the orders of Lieut. & Quartermaster Druce, 10th Hussars.

   (b) Brigade H.Qrs Royal Horse Guards, 8th M.G.Squadron, 20th M.V.S. at cross roads 200x S. of HALLOY CHURCH at 9.30 a.m. and march under Brigade Transport Officer.

4. Cyclists will march under Regimental arrangements.

5. All troops are to be N. of the DOULLENS – ARRAS road by 10 a.m.

6. Billeting parties will meet Staff Captain as under:-

   (a) 10th Hussars, Essex Yeomanry, 8th C.F.A. at REBREUVIETTE CHURCH at 9.45 a.m.

   (b) Royal Horse Guards and 8th M.G.Squadron at W in WAMIN at 10.15 a.m.

7. Acknowledge.

Capt,

4/7/17.   for Brigade Major, 8th Cavalry Brigade.

MARCH TABLE FOR JULY 5th, 1917.

Unit.	Starting Point.	Time.	Route.	Destination.	Billeting guides.	Remarks.
Brigade H.Q. 8th Sig. Trp.	As for R.H.G.	9.15 a.m.	As for R.H.Gds	ETREE-WAMIN.	At X roads just W. of ETREE-WAMIN STATION.	
R.Horse Gds.	X roads ½ mile S.W. of H in HALLOY.	8.45 a.m.	X roads L'ESPERANCE - LUCHEUX - 2nd U of LUCHEUX - W. side of BEAUDRICOURT.	ETREE-WAMIN.	As for Bde H.Q.	
8th M.G.Sqdn.	T. roads ½ mile S.W. of HALLOY CHURCH.	9.0 a.m.	W. of HALLOY - X rds L'ESPERANCE - L of LUCHEUX - IVERGNY - OPPY.	ETREE WAMIN.	W of WAMIN.	Not to debouch on to HALLOY - LUCHEUX rd till R.H.G. have passed.
10th Hussars.	T roads just S. of A in AUTHIEULE.	9.0 a.m.	DOULLENS - S of R. GROUCHES - GROUCHES E. side of BREVILLERS.	REBREUVIETTE.	X. roads just S. of REBREUVIETTE Church.	
Essex Yeo.	As for X.R.H.	8.30 a.m.	As for X.R.H.	REBREUVIETTE.	As for X.R.H.	
8th C.F.A.	W. end of PRESCHEVILLERS.	9.0 a.m.	S. of AUTHIE RIVER - DOULLENS - S. of GROUCHES H. - E. side of BREVILLERS.	REBREUVIETTE.	As for X.R.H.	Not to cross AUTHIE R. till X.R.H. are clear of the DOULLENS - AUTHIEULE Railway.
20th M.V.S.	As for Bde H.Q.	9.20 a.m.	As for Bde H.Q.	ETREE WAMIN.	As for Bde H.Q.	

APP. E

Royal Horse Guards,　　　　　　20th M.V.S.,
10th Royal Hussars,　　　　　　 8th Signal Troop,
Essex Yeomanry,　　　　　　　　Staff Captain,
8th M.G.S.,　　　　　　　　　　 Camp Commandant,
8th C.F.A.,　　　　　　　　　　 Supply Officer,
Brigade Transport Officer.　　 3rd Cav., Div., (for inf'n.)

Map ref: 1/100,000 LENS.

1. The Brigade will march tomorrow July 6th to a billeting area BOURS – CHAMET – GRICOURT – NOYELLES – MONNEVILLE – MAREST – DIEVAL – VALHOUN – LE HAMEL – ANTIN – ANTIGNEUL CHATEAU – BRITEL and GROSSART, in accordance with attached March Table. This area will be the final destination.

2. The Brigade (including 'B' Echelon) will be North of the ST. POL – BRUAY Road by 10 a.m.

3. 'A' Echelons will march in rear of units under an Officer to be detailed by each.

4. 'B' Echelons will march independantly by the same routes as their Units under an Officer to be detailed by each Unit.
'B' Echelons must give way to fighting troops.

5. Cyclists will march under Regimental arrangements.

6. A distance of 500 yards will be maintained in rear of each Regiment, Machine Gun Squadron and C.F.A.

7. Allotment of billets in new area will be forwarded this evening.

　　　　　　　　　　　　　　　　　　　　　　Eu Fulden　　Capt,
5th July 1917.　　　　　　Brigade Major, 8th Cavalry Brigade.

MOVEMENT TABLE FOR JULY 6th, 1917.

Unit.	Starting Point.	Time.	Route.	Remarks.
R. Horse Gds.	BERLENCOURT Church.	6.0 a.m.	MAIZIERES – AVERDOINGT – BAILLEUL-AUX-CORNAILLES – X roads 1000 S. of ANTIGNEUL Chateau.	
10th Hussars.	Road junction 500x E. of last T. of CANETTEMONT.	5.0 a.m.	NOUVIN-HOUVIGNEUL – ST. POL – VALHUON.	
Essex Yeo.	ETREE-WAMIN Church 1000x S. of B of SERLENCOURT.	6.0 a.m.	MAGNICOURT-sur-CANCHE – GOUY-EN-TERNOIS – FOUFFLIN-RICAMETZ – ROELLICOURT – BRYAS.	
8th M.G.Sqdn.	Same as Essex Yeo.	6.10 a.m.	Same as Essex Yeomanry.	Not to block R.H.G. or E.Yeo at ETREE-WAMIN – follow E.Yeo 'A' Echelon.
8th C.F.A.	Same as X.R.H.	6.10 a.m.	Same as X.R.H.	Follow X.R.H. 'A' Echelon.
Brigade H.Q. 8th Sig.Trp.	Same as R.H.G.	6.10 a.m.	Same as R.H.G.	Follow R.H.G. 'A' Echelon.
20th M.V.S.	Same as R.H.G.	6.15 a.m.	Same as R.H.G.	Follow Brigade Headquarters.

APP. F.

Royal Horse Guards,   8th Signal Troop,
10th Royal Hussars,   Staff Captain,
Essex Yeomanry,   Camp Commandant,
'G' Battery, R.H.A.   Supply Officer,
8th M.G.Squadron,   Capt. Baker, i/c B.Echelon,
8th C.F.A.   2/Lieut. Slim, X.R.H.i/o
20th M.V.S.   Brigade Cyclists
    3rd Cavalry Division. (For information)

=-=-=-=-=-=-=-=-=-=-=-=-=-=

B.M. 275/1.

Ref. Maps 1/100,000 LENS & HAZEBROUCK,
     1/40,000 Sheet 36a.

1. The 8th Cavalry Brigade will march to and concentrate in the area THIENNES - TANNAY - LE BRAY - HOULERON - PLAINE BAS - PLAINE HAUTE on July 17th in accordance with attached march table.

2. All movements will be completed by 10 a.m. The Brigade, including 'B' Echelon, will be clear of cross roads ½ mile N.W. of CAUCHY-A-LA-TOUR by 6 a.m.

3. 'A' Echelons will march in rear of units under an officer to be detailed by each unit.

4. 'B' Echelons will follow their units to the starting point giving way to fighting troops if necessary on route. On arrival at the Starting Point they will come under the orders of Captain BAKER, A.S.C. They will pass the Starting Point in order of march of Units at 6 a.m.

5. All Brigade Cyclists will be at the Starting Point at 5.5 a.m. where they will come under the orders of 2/Lieut. J.P.SLIM, 10th Royal Hussars.

6. After passing the Starting Point a distance of 500 yards will be maintained in rear of each Regiment, Battery and M.G.Squadron, and C.F.A.

7. Sick horses and any led horses with 'B' Echelon will march in rear of 'B' Echelon under Capt. FETHERSTONHAUGH, A.V.C. in order of march of Units.

8. The Staff Captain will meet billeting parties at THIENNES Church at 2.30 p.m. tomorrow 16th inst. Billeting parties will arrange to bivouac tomorrow night in new area.

9. On arrival in new billeting area Brigade Headquarters will be at THIENNES.

15/7/17.

Capt,
Brigade Major, 8th Cavalry Brigade.

MARCH TABLE FOR JULY 17th.

Unit.	Starting Point	Time.	Route.	Billeting area.	Remarks.
Brigade H.Q. & 8th Sig.Troop.	FERFAY CHURCH.	5.10-a.m.	CAMBLAIN-CHATELAIN - CAUCHY-A-LA-TOUR - FERPAY - ST. HILAIRE - AIRE.	THIENNES.	
10th Hussars.	do.	5.10 a.m.	do.	TANNAY.	
Essex Yeomanry.	do.	5.20 a.m.	do.	THIENNES.	Follow X.R.H. to starting point.
Royal Horse Guards.	do.	5.30 a.m.	CAMBLAIN CHATELAIN - FERFAY ST. HILAIRE - HAM-EN-ARTOIS - ISBERGUES.	HOULERON.	Arrange to divert 'B' Echelon at ST. HILAIRE.
8th Machine Gun Sqdn.	do.	5.40 a.m.	PERNES - AUMERVAL - FERFAY - ST. HILAIRE - AIRE - THIENNES.	PLAINE BAS.	Not to block R.H.Gds at FERFAY.
'G' Battery, R.H.A.	do.	5.45 a.m.	AUMERVAL - FERFAY - ST. HILAIRE - HAM-EN-ARTOIS - ISBERGUES.	LE BRAY.	Give way to 8th M.G.S. on road to Starting Point.
8th C.F.A.	do.	5.50 a.m.	BOURS - PERNES - PERFAY - ST. HILAIRE - AIRE.	THIENNES.	
20th M.V.S.	do.	5.55 a.m.	Same as for Brigade H.Q.	THIENNES.	

Army Form C. 2118.

WAR DIARY
INTELLIGENCE SUMMARY.   20 Mb. Vety. Sec.
(Erase heading not required.)

Vol 30

Place	Date	Hour	Summary of Events and Information	Remarks and references to Appendices
THIENNES	1.8.17		Routine.	
"	2.8.17		Routine.	
"	3.8.17		Routine.	
"	4.8.17		Evacuated 7 horses AIRE to 22 Vety. Ho.	
"	5.8.17		Routine.	
"	6.8.17		Routine.	
"	7.8.17		Routine.	
"	8.8.17		Routine. Received orders that this Section would move 10.8.17.	
"	9.8.17		Packing up ready for the move – Bombed by enemy aeroplanes during night.	
"	10.8.17		Moved to HAM EN ARTOIS.	
HAM EN ARTOIS	11.8.17		Routine.	
"	12.8.17		Routine.	
"	13.8.17		Routine.	
"	14.8.17		Routine – 25 horses evacuated AIRE to 22 Vety Ho.	
"	15.8.17		Routine.	
"	16.8.17		Routine.	

Army Form C. 2118.

WAR DIARY
or
INTELLIGENCE SUMMARY.

20 Mobile Vety. Sec.

(Erase heading not required.)

Instructions regarding War Diaries and Intelligence Summaries are contained in F. S. Regs., Part II. and the Staff Manual respectively. Title pages will be prepared in manuscript.

Place	Date	Hour	Summary of Events and Information	Remarks and references to Appendices
HAM EN ARTOIS	17.8.17	Routine		AW
"	16.8.17	Routine		AW
"	19.8.17	Routine		AW
"	20.8.17	Routine		AW
"	21.8.17	Routine		AW
"	22.8.17	Routine	13 Horses evacuated AIRE to 22 Vety. Hos.	AW
"	23.8.17	Routine		AW
"	24.8.17	Routine		AW
"	25.8.17	Routine		AW
"	26.8.17	Routine		AW
"	27.8.17	Routine	6 Horses evacuated AIRE to 22 Vety Hos.	AW
"	28.8.17	Routine		AW
"	29.8.17	Routine	7 Horses evacuated AIRE to 22 Vety Hos.	AW
"	30.8.17	Routine		AW
"	31.8.17	Routine	S03 P.A. Sgt HARRIS evacuated to hospital	AW

WAR DIARY
INTELLIGENCE SUMMARY.

(Erase heading not required.)

Army Form C. 2118.

Instructions regarding War Diaries and Intelligence Summaries are contained in F. S. Regs., Part II. and the Staff Manual respectively. Title pages will be prepared in manuscript.

20 Mot Vety Sec. September 1917 Sheet 1

Vf 31

Place	Date	Hour	Summary of Events and Information	Remarks and references to Appendices
AKM. EN ARRAS	1-9-17		Moved into a new billet at SE 8054 Pte NOTTER J.H. rebored to Bn	
	2-9-17		Went to Er-Island Water Guard ST. OMER.	
	3-9-17		Three sick horses evacuated AIRE to 22 Vety Ho.	
	4-9-17		Routine	
"	4-9-17		Routine. 8 sick horses evacuated AIRE to 22 Vety Ho.	
"	5-9-17		Routine.	
"	6-9-17		Routine 11 sick animals evacuated AIRE to 22 Vety Ho.	
"	7-9-17		Routine	
"	8-9-17		16 cast horses evacuated AIRE to 22 Vety Ho	
"	9-9-17		Routine	
"	10-9-17		Routine. 503 Pte L/Cp HARRIS returned from Hospital.	
"	11-9-17		Routine	
"	12-9-17		Routine. 24 horses evacuated AIRE to 22 Vety Ho.	
"	13-9-17		Routine	
"	14-9-17		Routine 16 horses evacuated AIRE to 22 Vety Ho	

WAR DIARY
INTELLIGENCE SUMMARY

Army Form C. 2118.

(Erase heading not required.)

2/Mt. Vety. Sec.
September 1917. Sheet 2.

Place	Date	Hour	Summary of Events and Information	Remarks and references to Appendices
NAM. EN ARDS.	15-9-17	Routine	SE 28431 Pte HUTTON J. admitted for duty from 2 Vety Hos.	
"	16-9-17	Routine		
"	17-9-17	Routine		
"	18-9-17	Routine		
"	19-9-17	Routine		
"	20-9-17	Routine		
"	21-9-17	Routine		
"	22-9-17	Routine	19 sick horses evacuated AIRE to 22 Vety Hos.	
"	23-9-17	Routine		
"	24-9-17	Routine		
"	25-9-17	Routine		
"	26-9-17	Routine		
"	27-9-17	Routine		
"	28-9-17	Routine		
"	29-9-17	Routine	14 sick horses evacuated AIRE to 22 Vety Hos.	
"	30-9-17	Routine		

WAR DIARY
INTELLIGENCE SUMMARY.

Army Form C. 2118.

October 1917

20 Mobile Vety. Section.

Vol 32

Place	Date	Hour	Summary of Events and Information	Remarks and references to Appendices
HAM EN ARTOIS	1.10.17		Routine	
"	2.10.17		Routine	OR
"	3.10.17		Routine	OR
"	4.10.17		Routine	OR
"	5.10.17		Routine	OR
"	6.10.17		22 sick horses evacuated AIRE to 22 Vety H⁰	OR
"	7.10.17		Routine	OR
"	8.10.17		9 sick horses evacuated AIRE to 22 Vety H⁰	OR
"	9.10.17		Routine	OR
"	10.10.17		Routine. 3 sick horses evacuated AIRE to 22 Vety H⁰	OR
"	11.10.17		Moved to Bivouac in RUE DE GUARBECQUE	APP. A.
RUE DE GUARBECQUE	12.10.17		Routine	OR
"	13.10.17		Routine	OR
"	14.10.17		Routine	OR
"	15.10.17		Routine - Personnel & animals AIRE to 22 Vety H⁰	OR
"	16.10.17		Routine - Received orders to move next day	OR

October 1917

Army Form C. 2118.

WAR DIARY
or
INTELLIGENCE SUMMARY.
20 Mt. Vety. Sec.

(Erase heading not required.)

Instructions regarding War Diaries and Intelligence Summaries are contained in F. S. Regs., Part II. and the Staff Manual respectively. Title pages will be prepared in manuscript.

Place	Date	Hour	Summary of Events and Information	Remarks and references to Appendices
RUE DE GUARBECQUE	17.10.17	6 A.M.	Moved M/S to starting point & proceeded via LILLERS and PERNES to PRESSY LES PERNES - An march easy - Arrived in the P.M.	APP. B.
PRESSY LES PERNES	18.10.17		Resting	
"	19.10.17		Resting. The Sick animals evacuated.	
"	20.10.17		Received orders for move following day.	
"	21.10.17	9.15 a.m.	Moved off to starting point & proceeded to REBREUVE in accordance with march table attached	APP. C.
REBREUVE		2.30 p.m.	Arrived in billets - Horses then under cover.	
"	22.10.17	9 a.m.	Moved off & proceeded via BOUVIGMAISON, HEM, MONTRELET to VIGNACOURT.	APP. D.
"		3 p.m.	Arrived in billets - All horses then under cover.	
VIGNACOURT	23.10.17		Resting.	
"	24.10.17		Resting.	
"	25.10.17		Resting.	
"	26.10.17		Resting.	
"	27.10.17		Resting.	
"	28.10.17		Resting.	

WAR DIARY
INTELLIGENCE SUMMARY

Army Form C. 2118.

October 1917

20th Mtd Vety Sec

Place	Date	Hour	Summary of Events and Information	Remarks and references to Appendices
VIGNACOURT	29.10.17		Strength 11 Horses CANADAS 6 21/WYTHS	
"	30.10.17		Ditto.	
"	31.10.17		Ditto.	

R Bruce McKenzie
20 Mtd Vety Sec

APP. A

S E C R E T.

Copy No. 8.

8th CAVALRY BRIGADE ORDER No. 4.

Reference map 5a Hazebrouck, 1/100,000
and Sheet 36a 1/40,000.   10th October, 17.

1. 8th Cavalry Brigade Order No.3 of 7/10/17 is cancelled.

2. 8th Cavalry Brigade will move tomorrow 11th inst., from
   HOLINGHEM - HAM-EN-ARTOIS - BERGUETTE area to the area
   about ROBECQ - ST. VENANT in accordance with march table
   overleaf.
   The Brigade will be North of the line Mt. BERNENCHON -
   GUARBECQUE by 12 noon.

3. Royal Horse Guards will remain at ROBECQ.

4. A. and B. Echelon will march in rear of their units, each
   under an officer to be detailed by units concerned.
   B. echelon will give way to fighting troops.

5. On arrival in new area Brigade Headquarters will be on the
   GUARBECQUE - ST. VENANT road about 1 mile E. of ST. VENANT
   (P.8.b.).

6. Acknowledge.

Issued at 3.45 pm   Ea Fulden   Capt,
                               Brigade Major, 8th Cavalry Brigade.

Copies No 1 - 7 normal issue.

    8. 20th A.V.S.
    9. 8th Signal Troop.
   10. Camp Commandant.
   11. Supply Officer.
   12. 3rd Cav. Divn.

MARCH TABLE FOR OCTOBER 11th, 1917.

Unit.	Starting Point.	Time of passing S.P.	Route.	Billeting area.
Brigade H.Qrs. 8th Signal Troop.	Road junction 200x N.E. of HAM Church.	10.40 a.m.	No restriction.	Rue de GUARBECQUE, East of cross roads at p.2.c.3.0.
10th Hussars.	BERGUETTE Station.	10.15 a.m.	"	Rue de GUARBECQUE, West of cross roads at P.2.c.3.0 & HAMET BILLET.
Essex Yeomanry.	Eastern exits of BERGUETTE.	10.0 a.m.	"	BAS HAMEL, HARTE VERT.
8th M.G.Squadron.	Road junction 200x N.E. of HAM CHURCH.	10.30 a.m.	"	LES AUSOIRES.
8th C.F.A.	do.	10.45 a.m.	"	ASILE D'ALIENES.
20th M.V.S.	do.	10.50 a.m.	"	RUE de GUARBECQUE. (with Bde H.Qrs).

APP. B.

SECRET.   Copy No. 8

8th CAVALRY BRIGADE ORDER No. 5.

Reference map 5a Hazebrouck & Lens. 1/100000   October 16th, 1917.

1. 8th Cavalry Brigade (less 'G' Battery, R.H.A.) will march tomorrow 17th inst to the PERNES area in accordance with march table overleaf.

2. The Brigade will be South of the Canal D'AIRE by 7.0 a.m. and South of the ESTREE BLANCHE - CAMBLAIN CHATELAIN Road by 10.45 a.m.

3. A distance of 500x will be maintained between units.

4. 'A' Echelons will follow units to the Starting Point where they will halt at the side of the road and allow Units to pass. 'A' Echelons will be Brigaded under Capt. V.T.G.Hine, Essex Yeo and will follow 20th M.V.S. in order of march of Units.

5. 'B' Echelons will follow units to the Starting Point where they will be Brigaded under Capt. E.J.Baker, A.S.C. They will pass the Starting Point in order of march of units at 7.0 a.m.

6. All Brigade Cyclists will be at the Starting Point at 6.10 a.m. where they will come under the orders of Lieut. Hughes, 10th Royal Hussars.

7. Allotment of billets in new area will follow.

8. Commanders of Echelons will arrange to divert Echelons of units to billets after passing PERNES.

9. ACKNOWLEDGE.

Issued at 2.45 p.m.
                                    T.A. Fulden   Capt,
                                Brigade Major, 8th Cavalry Brigade.

Copies 1 - 7 normal issue.
        8. 20th M.V.S.   12. Capt. V.T.G.Hine, E.Y.
        9. 8th Signal Troop.   13. Capt. E.J.Baker, A.S.C.
       10. Camp Commandant,   14. Lieut. Hughes, X.R.H.
       11. Supply Officer,   15th 3rd Cav. Divn.

MARCH TABLE - OCTOBER 17th, 1917.

STARTING POINT.   -   BUSNES Church.
ROUTE.   -   LILLERS - PERNES.

Unit.	Time of passing S.P.	Remarks.
Brigade H.Q. & 8th Signal Troop.	6.15 a.m.	
Royal Horse Guards.	6.15 a.m.	
10th Royal Hussars.	6.22 a.m.	Follow R.H.Gds through ROBECQ.
Essex Yeomanry.	6.29 a.m.	
8th M.G. Squadron.	6.36 a.m.	Not to block E.Y. on route to Starting Point.
8th C.F.A.	6.41 a.m.	
20th M.V.S.	6.46 a.m.	
A. Echelon.	6.50 a.m.	

APP. C

S E C R E T.　　　　　　　　　　　　　　　　　　　　　　　　Copy No. 8.

8th CAVALRY BRIGADE ORDER NO. 6.

Reference map LENS 1/100,000.　　　　　　　　　　　October 20th, 1917.

1.　8th Cavalry Brigade (less 'G' Battery, R.H.A.), 3rd Field Squadron, R.E. and No.2 Section 3rd Cavalry Reserve Park will march tomorrow 21st instant to the FREVENT area in accordance with march table overleaf.
　　　The march will be continued on 22nd inst to the CANAPLES area.

2.　After passing the Starting Point units may march independantly, but they will inform units in rear when they intend to halt etc,. A distance of at least 500x will be maintained between units.

3.　'A' Echelons will follow units to the Starting Point, where they will halt at the side of the road. 'A' Echelons will be Brigaded under Capt. V.T.G.Hine, Essex Yeomanry and will follow 20th M.V.S. in order of march.

4.　'B' Echelons will follow units to the Starting Point when they will be Brigaded under Capt. E.W.Baker, A.S.C. They will follow 3rd Field Squadron R.E. in order of march.

5.　All Brigade cyclists will be at the Starting Point at 9.55 a.m. where they will come under the orders of Lieut. Hughes, X.R.H.

6.　Commanders of Echelons will arrange to divert Echelons of Units to billets after passing ST. POL.

7.　On arrival in FREVENT area Brigade Headquarters will be at BREUVE.

8.　ACKNOWLEDGE.

　　　　　　　　　　　　　　　　　　　　　　　　　　　　　　Capt,
Issued at 10.30 a.m.　　　　　　　　　Brigade Major, 8th Cavalry Brigade.

Copies to 1 - 7 normal issue.
　　8.　20th M.V.S.　　　　　　　　13.　No.2 Section, 3rd Cavalry
　　9.　8th Signal Troop.　　　　　　　　Reserve Park.
　10.　Camp Commandant.　　　　14.　Capt. V.T.G.Hine, E.Y.
　11.　Supply Officer.　　　　　15.　Capt. E.W.Baker, A.S.C.
　12.　3rd Field Sqdn R.E.　　　16.　Lieut. Hughes, X.R.H.
　　　　　　　　　　　　　　　　17.　3rd Cavalry Division.

MARCH TABLE OCTOBER 21st, 1917.

Starting Point, Road Junction 100X E. of VALHUON Church.
Route - ST. POL.

Unit.	Time of passing S.P.	Billeting area.	Information.	Remarks.
Brigade H.Q. & 8th Sig: Troop.	10.0 a.m.	REBREUVE.		
10th Hussars.	10.0 a.m.	LIGNY-SUR-CANCHE - BOUBERS-SUR-CANCHE - FREVENT.	Town Major, FREVENT.	
Essex Yeo.	10.7 a.m.	VAMIN - ETREE VAMIN - REBREUVIETTE - ROZIERE - BROUILLY - CANETTEMONT.	Billot Warden REBREUVIETTE.	Not to block 2 Sqdns K.R.H. billeted at CAMBLAIN CHATELAIN en route to S.P.
R.Horse Gds.	10.14 a.m.	CONCHY-SUR-CANCHE - MONCHEL - VACQUERIE-LE-BOUCQ - PORT.	Area Commdt. ROUBEAU.	
8th M.G. Sqdn.	10.21 a.m.	SIBIVILLE - SERICOURT - HERNAL.	Area Commdt. ST. POL.	Remain clear of PERNES - ST. POL main road till tail of R.H.G. has passed.
8th C.F.A.	10.26 a.m.	HOUVIN - HOUVIGNEUL.		
20th M.V.S.	10.31 a.m.	REBREUVE.	Maire.	
A. Echelons.	10.35 a.m.			
3rd Field Sqdn R.E.	10.40 a.m.	PETIT BOURET - Gd.BOURET.	Billet Warden REBREUVIETTE.	Not to block K.R.H. & E.Y. on route to S.P.
B. Echelons.	10.50 a.m.			
No.2 Sec. 3rd Cav.Res.Park.	11.0 a.m.	BONNIERES.	Area Commdt. BOUBERS.	

APP. D

SECRET.   Copy No. 8.

8th CAVALRY BRIGADE ORDER No. 7.

Reference maps LENS & AMIENS 1/100,000.   October 20th, 1917.

1.   8th Cavalry Brigade (less 'G' Battery, R.H..), 3rd Field Squadron, R.E. and No.2 Section 3rd Cavalry Reserve Park will march on 22nd inst from the FREVENT area to the CANAPLES area in accordance with march table overleaf.
   A distance of at least 500% will be maintained between units.

2.   'A' Echelons will march in rear of units under an officer to be detailed by each unit.

3.   'B' Echelons will march independantly by the same routes as their units under an officer to be detailed by each unit.
   'B' Echelons must give way to faster moving troops if required.

4.   On arrival in CANAPLES area Brigade Headquarters will be at VIGNACOURT.

5.   ACKNOWLEDGE.

                                       ExFilden   Capt,
Issued at   Brigade Major, 8th Cavalry Brigade.

Copies 1 - 7 normal issue.   11. Supply Officer,
      8. 20th M.V.S.   12. 3rd Field Squadron. R.E.
      9. 8th Signal Troop,   13. No.2 Section, 3rd Cavalry
     10. Camp Commandant,   Reserve Park.
                                    14. 3rd Cavalry Division.

Allotment of billets attached.

MARCH TABLE, OCTOBER 22nd, 1917.

Unit.	Starting Point.	Time of passing S.P.	Route.	Remarks.
Brigade H.Q. 8th Sig.Tep.	Southern exit of REBREUVE.	9.15 a.m.	BOUQUEMAISON - HEM MONTRELET.	
A Horse Gun.	Under Regimental arrangements.		FROHEN-LE-GRAND - BERNAVILLE - DOMART-EN-PONTHIEU.	
10th Hussars.	Southern exit of BEHIERES.	9.16 a.m.	BARLY - FIENVILLERS.	
Essex Yeo.	Under Regimental Arrangements.		LUCHEUX - DOULLENS - BEAUVAL.	
8th M.G. Sqn.	Southern exit of MONVAL.	8.45 a.m.	REBREUVE - BOUQUEMAISON - HEM - CANDAS - MONTRELET.	
8th C.F...	1st 2 of HOUVIN MOUVIGNEUL.	9.0 a.m.	REBREUVIETTE - HEM - CANDAS MONTRELET.	
20th M.V.S.	Southern exit of REBREUVE.	9.20 a.m.	Same as for Bde H.Q.	
3rd Field Sqn. R.E.	Southern exit of Gd BOURET.	10.0 a.m.	HEM - CANDAS - MONTRELET.	
No. 2 Sec. 3rd Cav. Res. Park.	Southern exit of BONNIERES.	9.40 a.m.	BARLY - FIENVILLERS.	

Army Form C. 2118.

20th Mobile Veterinary Section. WAR DIARY or INTELLIGENCE SUMMARY.

November 1917.

Sheet 1.

VM 33

Instructions regarding War Diaries and Intelligence Summaries are contained in F. S. Regs., Part II. and the Staff Manual respectively. Title pages will be prepared in manuscript.

(Erase heading not required.)

Place	Date	Hour	Summary of Events and Information	Remarks and references to Appendices
VIGNACOURT	5th		20 sick horses evacuated CANDAS to 22 Vety Hospital.	
"	6th		CAPT. R. T. FORREST A.V.C. arrived to take over command 20 M.V.S.	
"	8th		CAPT. R. J. FORREST A.V.C. assumed command 20 M.V.S. from CAPT. T. T. DAVIS A.V.C.	
"	11th		CAPT. T. J. DAVIS and SE 3211 Pte WELBY proceeded to 4 Vety Hospital CALAIS.	
"	12th		21 sick horses evacuated CANDAS to 22 Vety Hospital.	
"	16th		Ordered to move to BRAY on night 18/11/17.	
"	17th		Evacuated 12 horses by road to 22 Vety Hospital, also 14 M.V.S.	
"	18th		3 sick animals left at VIGNACOURT	
BRAY	22nd		Moved to BRAY. 3 sick animals evacuated sick	
"	"		Pte R. E. BUCHANAN evacuated sick	
"	23rd		Moved to BERTANGLES.	
BERTANGLES	26th		Cavalry Corps Motor Float attached for duty.	
"	27th		Collected 3 sick horses left at VIGNACOURT 18/11/17. 2 evacuated in Cavalry Corps	
"	"		Motor float to 22 Vety Hospital	
"	29th		14 sick horses evacuated BELLE EGLISE to 22 Vety Hospital. Cavalry Corps	
"	"		Float returned to Cavalry Corps.	

8/12/17

R. J. Forrest Capt.
O.C. 20 M.V.S.

Army Form C. 2118.

20th Mobile Veterinary WAR DIARY December 1917
Section INTELLIGENCE SUMMARY.
(Erase heading not required.)

Sheet 1.

Place	Date	Hour	Summary of Events and Information	Remarks and references to Appendices
BERTANGLES	2nd		Moved to BELLOY-SUR-SOMME.	
BELLOY	18th		Evacuated one Charger of MAJOR GENERAL J. VAUGHAN CB. DSO by road to 14 Veterinary Hospital, ABBEVILLE.	
	25th		No. SE29984 PTE ASHLEY. R.W. joined section from No. 7 Veterinary Hospital.	

10/1/18 R Ponsonby Capt
O.C. 20 M.V.S.

20th Mobile Veterinary Section

WAR DIARY
INTELLIGENCE SUMMARY
(Erase heading not required.)

January 1918 Army Form C. 2118.
WD 35 Sheet 1

Place	Date	Hour	Summary of Events and Information	Remarks and references to Appendices
BELLOY SUR SOMME	Jan 3rd		40 SE 3211 Pte WELBY.W. joined section from No 4 Veterinary Hospital.	
"	9th		15 sick horses evacuated by road to No 14 Veterinary Hospital	
"	11th		40 SE 3999. Pte TAMBLIN.F.E. despatched to No 12 Veterinary Hospital	
"	14th		37 horses cast by D.D.V.R. evacuated to No 14 Veterinary Hospital.	
"	21st		22 sick horses evacuated by road to No 14 Veterinary Hospital.	
"	26th		6 sick horses evacuated by road to No 14 Veterinary Hospital.	
"	27th		Moved to MARGELCAVE	
MARCELCAVE	28th		Moved to MIRANCOURT	

20th Mobile Veterinary Section   February 1918   Army Form C. 2118.

WAR DIARY
INTELLIGENCE SUMMARY
(Erase heading not required.)

Vol 36 Sheet 1.

Place	Date	Hour	Summary of Events and Information	Remarks and references to Appendices
N.E. RAUCOURT	10		40 SE 15333. S.S. BLICK R reported for duty from No 10 Vety Hospital.	
N.E. RAUCOURT	12		Evacuated 26 sick animals from TINCOURT to No 7 Vety Hospital.	
"	19		Evacuated 13 sick animals from TINCOURT to No 7 Vety Hospital.	
"	22		57B2208 Pte SHARPIN.W.M. and 5E3993 Pte TAMBLIN F.E. reported for duty from No 2 Vety Hospital.	
"	23		57055 SE 4648 Pte BRYANT F.G. and SE3864 Pte SMITH F.C. reported to No 2 Vety Hospital.	
"	24		No SE 3063 Pte WINSON R.I. despatched to No 2 Vety Hospital	
"	25		No SE 2789 P/A Cpl SMITH.W. returned from No 9 Vety Hospital for duty.	
"	26		Evacuated 23 sick animals from TINCOURT to No 7 Vety Hospital.	

A J Farrier Capt
O.C. 20 M V S.
10/3/18.